Other books by Thomas L. Quick

POWER, INFLUENCE,
& YOUR EFFECTIVENESS
IN HUMAN RESOURCES

POWER, INFLUENCE, & YOUR EFFECTIVENESS IN HUMAN RESOURCES

Thomas L. Quick

ADDISON-WESLEY PUBLISHING COMPANY, INC.
Reading, Massachusetts   Menlo Park, California   New York
Don Mills, Ontario   Wokingham, England   Amsterdam
Bonn   Sydney   Singapore   Tokyo   Madrid   San Juan

Library of Congress Cataloging-in-Publication Data

Quick, Thomas L.
  Power, influence, and your effectiveness in human
  resources/Thomas L. Quick.
    p.   cm.
  ISBN 0-201-06649-1
  1. Personnel management.   2. Organizational
  effectiveness.   3. Power (Social sciences)
  4. Influence (Psychology)   I. Title
HF5549.Q53 1988   658.3 — dc19   87-33001

Cover design by Mike Fender
Text design by Carson Design
Set in 11 point Palatino by Compset, Inc., Beverly, MA

ABCDEFGHIJ-DO-898
First Printing, April 1988.

To Prudy Scordino

Executive Director of the New York Metro chapter, ASTD

Contents

PREFACE

Power is a high priority issue among human resources people. I didn't realize that in 1984, when the publishing house of Franklin Watts asked me to do a book on power in organizations. I hadn't written much on the subject before, even though I had a number of scars testifying that I had climbed into the ring. In fact, my twenty-one-year career at the Research Institute of America (RIA) had come to an end a short time before, in part due to power issues. So I knew something about the subject.

The summer that my book *Power Plays* came out (New York: Franklin Watts, 1985), I had a casual conversation with a veteran of the training scene, in which I talked about what I like about trainers. I've always believed that as a group they are more intelligent and interesting than the general population. "I like to work with them and I like to party with them," I said. He nodded and asked what I disliked about trainers. "They see themselves as powerless," I answered. Again he nodded.

That conversation sparked a few thoughts about human resources professionals being a readily-identifiable market for any presentations I might care to give on the subject of power. When I was asked soon after to speak before some chapters of the American Society for Training and Development (ASTD), I suggested "Power, Influence, and Your Effectiveness" as a topic. My premise that trainers tend to see themselves as powerless was reinforced by every audience.

I gave the presentation in Atlanta in June 1987 at the ASTD National Conference, and about five times as many people as I had expected showed up. Even more tried to get into the jammed room. Power is indeed a priority issue.

Thus, when Addison-Wesley approached me to do a book, I suggested the same subject. But I also suggested that we market the book to all human resources professionals, since staff people everywhere share a feeling of powerlessness, especially when compared to line management.

The twelve sources or kinds of power that I identified for *Power Plays*, the forerunner of this book, have stood the test of time and examination. But during my presentations, I came to realize that human resources professionals aren't just interested in learning what kinds of power are available—they want to know how to draw on them to build a power base. Many trainers, having come from the public sector, are not politically savvy. It may be true that some disdain power and politics, but I suspect it is more true that most human resources people are seeking more influence than they presently enjoy. This book, therefore, is not merely expository; it is a how-to as well.

How valid are trainers' perceptions of themselves as powerless? In some cases, no doubt, quite valid. It reminds me of an old joke. A fellow came to a psychiatrist, saying, "I have an inferiority complex." The therapist agreed to take him on. After a few sessions, he announced to the patient, "I wish to reassure you that you do not have an inferiority complex. You are, in fact, inferior." Some trainers *are* without influence in their organizations, and there may be little or nothing they can do about their situations. But others have influence and don't use it. They seem happy to remain reactive, to go along with whatever management wants. They do nothing to build a base of professional respect and credibility. I don't waste much grief on these people when, in times of cutbacks, they are declared expendable by management.

But whether or not human resources professionals need or want more power and influence on their own, they can expect to come under increasing pressure by management to do so. That may sound ironic. In the professionals' minds, management has withheld power. But the same management may well chastise the professionals for not exercising it.

Andrew S. Grove, president of Intel Corporation (and author of *High Output Management*, Random House 1983), wrote a provocative article about three years ago for the *Wall Street Journal* entitled "Is anyone Minding the Monitors?" You and I are the monitors. We make up, in Grove's terms, the "human-resource organization." To any human resources professional's delight, Grove asserts that any organization that struggles with competition, change, and stress, and operates "in the real world, with flesh-and-blood managers who are less than perfect," needs a human-resource organization.

But vital as we are, Grove charges that we "fall quite short of discharging" our duties. The reason: the "Pollyanna syndrome." We don't "call a spade a spade." When confronted with management misdeeds, we often prefer, Grove says, to look the other way. He identifies three important areas in which too frequently we do less than our best:

1. *Training.* Many managers are shortsighted: They don't want to spare their subordinates for training that takes them away from their desks and work stations.

2. *Objectives.* Managers have trouble setting realistic objectives, especially when those objectives will displease the boss. So they establish unrealistic objectives that look good but set employees up for failure.

3. *Rewards.* Managers say they reward good performance, but in truth they promote and compensate people on the basis of seniority alone.

And, according to Grove, what do we human resources folks do in the presence of these counterproductive managerial behaviors? Usually nothing. We know they're wrong, but we plead that we don't have the authority to do anything about them. Grove goes further. He suggests that we are happy not having the authority and thus the obligation to correct such practices. We are, to use the vernacular, wimps.

When I read the Grove article, I expected to hear an outcry of rage from human resources people I knew. But I heard nothing. At first I said, "Well, they're avoiding the issue." But the truth is less psychological: I discovered that many trainers don't read the *Wall Street Journal* very often. In all likelihood the target population missed the barrage (and vice versa). One trainer did, however, grumble to me, "That's fine for a president to say."

The bad news for us in human resources is that Andrew Grove speaks for many executives. They really do expect us to do more. No, they will not hand us the power, they argue. It is there for us if we choose to take it, to earn it. While human resources professionals complain that they are not invited by management to participate—as they should—in setting both operational and strategic plans, management apparently sees no reason to issue invitations.

As a profession, we indeed have a wimpy image. We are seen as reactive, as order-takers, as followers. And we have credibility and authority problems. Too many managers seem to believe that our ability to provide effective help—outside of skills training, at any rate—is severly limited by our lack of knowledge of the real world, where, of course, *they* live.

Their opinions are shared, unfortunately, by many human resources professionals. In the recent past I've heard the following scornful statements from three veterans in training:

"There are so many trainers out there who know so little."

"I don't have much respect for many trainers I meet."

"This field is dominated by elementary school teachers."

When you work and associate with as many trainers as I have since I first became active in ASTD many years ago, you become familiar with the disdain that senior and high-level trainers exhibit for other trainers, and toward ASTD, which in their view is largely populated and controlled by "junior" people who merit little respect. In much of ASTD today, at the national as well as the chapter level, senior professionals insist on having their own groups separate from the rest. Elitism prevails.

In this book, I have addressed the issue of human resources professionals' wimpy image and lack of authority and credibility. I have simply repeated in print what I have said on numerous occasions to groups of human resources professionals, at all levels. But I don't waste much space lamenting the image and the issues. There are steps that each individual can take to get out from under this unfortunate image and to build power, influence, authority, and credibility. And I'm reasonably confident that you will find some of those steps described in this book.

The style of writing is what I would call presentational. It is as if I were making a presentation, and as such, is informal and discursive. I hope it is entertaining, as well.

People who attend my presentations get the following speech. It applies to this book as well:

> *"One of the rewards of growing old in this profession is that you move beyond the Moses complex. In any case, I no longer have to carry those heavy stone tablets down from the mountain. To be quite candid, God hasn't talked to me lately, at least about training. Therefore, what you're going to get are my biases. You can question them, argue against them, accept or reject them. And I hope you'll feel free to do any of the above."*

That disclaimer applies to everything I write in this book. So if you find yourself getting upset with anything I say, just think, "I don't agree with him." Take what you do agree with—and may it help you build your base of power and influence.

1

Your Perspectives on Power

Few of us who have been in organizational life are neutral on the subject of power. As I wrote in the beginning of *Power Plays*, "If that word [power] makes you uncomfortable, summons up great ambivalence, suggests something that is both desirable and fearsome, you are quite normal. Most people experience some conflict when they think about power. It can be seductive. It can be repulsive. It can be used, and, certainly, abused" (p. 1).

Most people in the average organization don't really believe they have much, if any, power. But they sense that if you want to achieve significant objectives, have influence on others, and get on the fast track, you must build a power base. In short, if you want to get anything done of any magnitude, you have to have power. At the same time, there is the belief, often not expressed, that in general the pursuit of power stamps one as being not "nice."

People who perceive themselves as powerless, relatively or totally, tend to disdain power. Again from *Power Plays*, "People who disdain power usually don't understand it, don't see themselves as having it, don't know how to go about getting it, and fear it in others. Their misunderstanding of power—and its legitimacy—robs them of achievement, and of satisfaction in their work and careers, and it contributes greatly to their frustrations and feelings of helplessness, of being controlled by events and others."

The following is a brief quiz in which you can give voice to your perceptions of power issues. It's probable that there are no absolutely right or wrong answers. But the answers I provide, against which you can match yours, are my perceptions of the issues. And my answers set the tone for what follows in this book. So I urge you not to bypass the quiz, but to take a few minutes with it before proceeding further.

	AGREE	DISAGREE	NOT SURE
1. Power comes from whom you know rather than from what you know.	☐	☐	☐
2. Anyone who works in an organization can acquire power.	☐	☐	☐
3. It is usually more correct to say that power is given to the power-seeker rather than that the power-seeker takes it.	☐	☐	☐
4. Subordinates are a good source of power for their managers.	☐	☐	☐
5. Power itself is neutral, neither good nor bad in itself.	☐	☐	☐
6. Credibility is essential to the maintenance of power.	☐	☐	☐
7. The power that flows from one's position on the organizational chart is the strongest kind of power, because it is sanctioned by the hierarchy.	☐	☐	☐

8. For people on the power track, that is, seeking to

	AGREE	DISAGREE	NOT SURE
build a power base, the ideal boss-subordinate relationship is collaborative.	☐	☐	☐
9. Sensitivity is a characteristic of many people on the power track.	☐	☐	☐
10. A failure can be a significant factor in acquiring power.	☐	☐	☐
11. It is generally true that a person's authority will not equal his or her responsibility in an organization.	☐	☐	☐
12. Information is power.	☐	☐	☐
13. Conflict, politics, and competition for power are inevitable in a vibrant, growing organization.	☐	☐	☐
14. A participative, consensus-seeking managerial style is antithetical to seeking or building power.	☐	☐	☐
15. Often, an effective way to build power inside an organization is from the outside.	☐	☐	☐
16. When powerful people become insensitive to others, they put their power base at risk.	☐	☐	☐

	AGREE	DISAGREE	NOT SURE

17. A management-by-negotiation style usually results in the manager's having to give up power. ☐ ☐ ☐

18. Human resources professionals are generally correct when they say that the sources or kinds of power available to them are much more limited than for line people. ☐ ☐ ☐

19. People in human resources can build power through extending rewards to others in the organization. ☐ ☐ ☐

20. Basic selling skills, such as those used routinely by professional salespeople, are useful for non-salespeople in creating influence. ☐ ☐ ☐

The answers that follow reveal what I have learned about or concluded on the subject in my thirty years of corporate life, and they reflect my biases, for which I take total responsibility.

1. Not sure. Some people work all their lives at knowing lots of people, and never enjoy any power as a result of it. I could probably make a case for "Disagree"—and for "Agree." Here's what I mean. There is, as I explain later, power that can be derived from association with powerful people. But without competence, the person who draws on that reflected power is in a highly precarious, usually temporary position. When the sponsor or power center is removed, there goes the associative power. If the beneficiary of associative power is competent, he or she may survive. If not, he or she generally won't. And I've seen some situations in which the person trying to bask in the reflected power was not very successful in building his or her own power base. Co-workers found ways to subtly sabotage the efforts to have power. As a flat statement, "Power comes from who you know" is a tenuous premise. I would prefer "Not sure," because real, substantial power usually also involves what you know—the exceptions, which we have all seen, notwithstanding.

2. Agree. Years ago I used to make what I now regard as a fatuous statement: power in an organization is finite—there is only so much of it. Thank heaven I live and learn. There is, in most organizations, plenty of power for the asking and taking. There are, as you'll see, so many different kinds and sources of power that it is conceivable to me that everyone could enjoy some of it. It's there, if you know where to look and how to use it. Unless you're working for an autocrat who forbids anyone else to exercise any real power, there is enough to go around.

3. Agree. Yes, we have all seen people who are quite ruthless (termed "Jungle Fighters" by Michael Maccoby, in his famous book *The Gamesman*)—if not in life then on television or in the movies. Predators invite other predators. When people perceive that you have "stolen" something from them, they find ways to rebel. It's also my perception that Jungle Fighters have to switch jungles from time to time, when they are successfully challenged. I suppose a case could be made for "Not sure," since some power seekers manage to intimidate others into giving up power to them. But taking power is not usually a secure and lasting way to enjoy it, once your adversaries start trying to get it back from you. Better to negotiate it by persuading people that it is in their best interest to let you have it.

4. Agree. When employees produce well, they provide some of the blocks for a manager's power foundation. High quantity and quality output earn managers points. Such a manager has resources that, presumably, the organization needs—the more and the better, the greater potential for power. Furthermore, the manager's demonstrated competence in managing a high-output operation can be a source of power as well. If such competence is in short supply in the organization, the potency potential is higher.

If the manager's department provides candidates for promotion to greater responsibility, that manager will eventually enjoy allies and collaborators throughout the organization.

5. *Agree.* Despite Lord Acton's warning that power corrupts, stick with agree.

6. *Agree.* The key word in the sentence is "maintenance." People who are liars and untrustworthy can gain and hold power for a time, but when they are found out, others begin to plot ways to erode that power. People will be more likely to let you have power if you say that you're going to do good things with it, and actually do. People who can't be believed lose their ability to influence others to work with them.

7. *Not sure,* verging on *Disagree.* Most human resources people wouldn't agree that their power flows from position, unless they report to the top and are formally vested with power, in which case what they enjoy, as I'll explain in detail, is a combination of position and assigned power. Some people in organizations have a great deal of position power, at least in the beginning—certainly a CEO or a president, or an executive in a fast-track or highly profitable function. But for most people, I suspect that position power must be supplemented by other kinds of power. And, of course, we all know that in many organizations the real power is found in the white spaces between the boxes.

8. *Agree.* It doesn't help you, if you're seeking power, to work under a boss who is competitive or niggardly about letting go of authority and responsibility. If you are fortunate to have something resembling a partnership with your boss, you make the boss look good, and working for that kind of person helps you. If both of you are seen as competent, there's glory for each. For you to make tracks, you have to have at least your boss's tacit encouragement. An actively collaborative arrangement is better.

9. *Agree.* If you answered "Disagree," I suggest that your definition of the word *"sensitivity"* is too narrow. Sensitivity is not to be described as wimpiness. The word is quite compatible with such adjectives as "hardheaded" and "pragmatic." What sensitivity denotes is an awareness of the needs, wants, and boundaries

of other people as well as of your own. People who are insensitive are poorly tuned in to others. Since there is a lot of give-and-take in building power, you cannot afford to be blindsided, as they say these days. If you want to be good in negotiating, persuading, and influencing, you have to make sure, as good salespeople do, that your "product" will meet the needs and wants of others. You must also be sure that in extending your boundaries you don't seriously threaten the boundaries and turf of others, especially if they have the power to do you harm. If you are a man who considers sensitivity on the work scene to be a feminine trait, know that he-men can develop sensitivity, too—and they had better.

10. Agree. Way back, about twenty years ago, I remember a famous consultant saying to me that "you can't know what you can do until you know what you can't do." However precisely he put it, his message, as I recall, was that you had to do some failing if you wanted to do some succeeding. To try and then to fail helps you fix boundaries. You may find that what you've tried is something that you shouldn't try again; you don't have the potential for making a go of it. Or you can try it again with training, practicing, or help. People who are good at building power generally come to know when they are overreaching themselves, putting their power and prestige at risk. There may be times to take the chance, times not to. But to evaluate the chances of success, they must have a good measure of themselves. So, yes, failure plays an important role in acquiring power, because it defines what you can and cannot do. You can't afford to take too many risks that can multiply your failures—not if you want to hold on to your power.

11. Agree. This is true unless you do everything yourself. The point is that in any organization, while you may have responsibility and accountability, you must still rely on others to help you achieve your goals. Even most CEOs would probably tell you that their authority does not match their responsibilities.

12. Not sure. This is a cliché. Everyone—almost everyone—accepts it as true. But I believe it's not what you know but how you use what you know that contributes to your power. If your information is to provide you power, you must be selective and discriminating in how and when you let go of it.

13. *Agree.* If an organization is fermenting, lots of things are going on, and they should be. People have different goals and different ways of achieving the same goals. Of course, management must maintain control. If management permits people to build empires, withhold cooperation, and try to do others in, nothing good will come of it. It's an issue of controlling and channeling, not stifling.

14. *Disagree.* When people participate in decisions that affect them, when they engage in consensus decision making, the result is not only better decisions but a commitment by all concerned to carry them out. Good decision making increases the perception of your competence in others, which in turn contributes to your power. And when you have a contract with others through consensus, you don't have to keep looking over your shoulder—or over theirs—to make sure they are following you.

15. *Agree.* You can engage in activities, such as leadership in a professional or community group, that will persuade your colleagues that you have a competence that extends beyond your working day. Furthermore, if you are valued by professionals or other managers outside your organization, people inside tend to believe you should be taken seriously.

16. *Agree.* When people who need to work through and with others cease to be aware of the wants and needs of those others, they lose their ability to influence them. Persuading people to accept your ideas, your projects, your leadership, and you yourself is a matter of showing them how such acceptance is in their best interests. People simply don't choose courses of action that don't produce some good for them. If the powerful person is no longer tuned in to what others regard as rewarding choices for them, he or she is operating somewhat blindly.

17. *Not Sure.* Sometimes a manager who negotiates with others gains more than he or she might have by trying to force or direct them. And if the negotiation produces a commitment on the part of those who have been party to it, then the manager could be said to have gained power. It's my belief that people give you power, or permit you to exercise it, primarily because they feel it is in their interests to do so. When you negotiate, you give others the opportunity to seek what they want or need. And if that process involves their committing themselves to you, you're more powerful than you were before negotiating. Of course, negotiation does not always produce a completely winning situation for the negotiator. On balance, however, I'd rely on a negotiation style to increase my power and influence.

18. Disagree. I believe that many human resources professionals feel this way. But, as you'll see in this book, there are sources and kinds of power available to almost anyone working in an organization, which people don't draw on as they might. Staff people may not enjoy the power that flows from a position on the organization chart. But most other sources are there for human resources people.

19. Agree. More on this later. If you have credibility and authority, your evaluation of others in the organization can carry substantial weight. But of course, you must be someone who is taken seriously.

20. Agree. Some years ago, when as a management specialist at the Research Institute of America I was advising members on how they could be more effective in influencing the people they worked with, I came to realize that many of my recommendations were based on basic selling skills that I had learned as a young man during my twelve years in the sales field. Most conversations and interactions that managers engage in are selling situations. Later in this book you'll see exactly what I mean.

If you agreed with my answers to all twenty questions, it means that you agree with my perceptions, and that your experiences parallel mine. It probably also indicates that you've acquired a few scars through the years from involvements in power issues. If you had problems with any of my answers, you'll find more elaborate explanations of many of the above points in the book that follows.

2

Becoming an Influencer

I suspect that the view of the in-house trainer as a salesperson is a relatively unpopular one. Probably few trainers would accept that role with great enthusiasm. Yet the reality is that trainers are sellers. They have products. They have prospects. As staff people, they make recommendations to those prospects. Even if the programs are mandated, trainers still have the obligation to persuade their prospects to accept what human resources professionals have to offer. After all, people can accept the mandate without having to buy what is mandated. People can go through training without letting themselves be trained.

Selling skills, influencing or persuading skills—whatever you'd like to call them—are in most cases a must for the trainer. Indeed, they are suitable skills for anyone in human resources.

Andrew Grove is probably right when he says that the authority is there for human resources people to draw on. But it isn't as easy as picking it up. It's more realistic to say that we have to negotiate for it. Sometimes we have to persuade management that it is in their best interests to permit us to act authoritatively.

The theme of this section, therefore, is persuasion and influence: how to become more skilled in persuading and influencing those with whom we work.

CHARACTERISTICS OF INFLUENTIAL PEOPLE

While it's true that nearly everyone is trying to sell something and to persuade others, it's also evident that some people are better at it than others. Several years ago, while doing a book on influencing called *The Persuasive Manager*, (Chilton, 1982), I identified eight characteristics that people who are good at getting results from others tend to possess. Here they are:

1. Influential people know what they want.
2. They know they have a right to try to get what they want.
3. They are articulate.
4. They are sensitive.
5. They have credibility.
6. They know how to deal with opposition.
7. They know how to ask for action—and do.
8. They know what motivates others.

Look around you at the people who seem most skilled at persuading others to accept their opinions, their ideas, their projects. You'll see many or all of the above characteristics at work. Remember that influence is power. The more influence, the greater the power. None of the above is a gift at birth; all can be developed.

1. Influential People Know What They Want. You ought to be able to define goals for the next one, three, and five years. Those goals have to be important to you, as opposed to reflecting the "shoulds" and "oughts" that others may try to impose on you. And the goals should be realistic. Can you achieve them without undue risk and effort? The best goals are those that offer a challenge but do not involve extraordinary effort or immoderate risk. People who set unrealistic goals often overreach themselves and project less than powerful images. It's important also to be flexible with respect to those goals. As you progress toward them, you may sense that they are too low and too easy, or that they are too complicated and risky. You can always make adjustments. But the overriding priority is that you always have goals.

Knowing what you want and where you're going are strong components of personal power. Such people are not indecisive.

In today's parlance, strong influencers own their wants and needs. In fact, in a broader sense, they own themselves. They have a keen sense of themselves—of their aptitudes, their strengths, their boundaries and limitations. They come across as knowing who they are and being confident of what they can do. There is unmistakable self-acceptance.

People who are strongly goal oriented but who are also influential have a need to win; although, because they want results from and through others, they know that they cannot consistently win at the expense of those others.

2. Influential People Know They Have a Right to Try to Get What They Want. I suspect that this second characteristic of influentials comes as a surprise to many people. The difference between those who are skilled at persuading and the general population is that the former know they have a right. The fact is that everyone does have the right. Of course, you don't have the right to get what you want. But the expert salesperson, a prime influencer, is—to use a sales term—assumptive. The assumption is that if the product is good and meets the prospect's needs, and if the salesperson tells a good story, the prospect will buy. But the good salesperson never confuses the assumption or probability with a "right" to get the order.

Much the same thing can be said of you. You may not necessarily have the right to get your plan approved, your solution accepted, your ideas adopted, or your promotion granted, but you certainly have the right to speak your mind, to offer yourself and your ideas, and to express your needs and wants.

Not only do you have the right to make known what you want and need, you probably should, regularly. If you can make a good case for what you want and need, you probably will not do yourself harm by asking for it. In fact, you increase your visibility. No matter how large or small your desire—more money in the budget or your own subscription to the *Wall Street Journal*—be vocal. You may get a yes. And with every yes comes a little bit more power. With every affirmation, your image as an influencer becomes sharper.

As you'll see later in another section on persuasion principles, you'll achieve greater and more frequent success in your selling if you show the people you're asking why it is to their benefit to let you have what you want.

3. *Influential People Are Articulate.* Some people ramble, taking a long time to organize their thoughts and to tell you the bottom line of their thinking. Other people start and stop, fumbling as they try to pick the thread of thought they want. Still others, like children, must start at the beginning and tell everything in sequence, as their listeners fret and wonder whether they will ever get to the point. Then there are the tactful and diplomatic people, who will say such things as, "I can well understand why you take such pride in this report. It is so thorough and well prepared that I believe you should be congratulated on the tremendous and thoughtful effort you have expended. I've always said that if anyone wants a conscientious piece of work, call on you. I'm troubled a little bit, however, by some of your conclusions. Do you mind if I run through some of them with you? After all, the report is so excellent, I wouldn't want it marred by a few inaccuracies or misunderstandings." After all that softening up, veterans of this type of exchange know that they are about to get a blow to the body. People who are less experienced walk out on a high, thinking they have just received fabulous positive feedback.

The point is that all of the above ways of communicating—or more properly, non-communicating—leave listeners wondering what the true message is. Does the speaker agree or disagree? Does the speaker support the idea or object to it? Does the person understand, or has he or she missed the target completely?

Most of us in organizational life are more accustomed to the rambler, the hesitater and stammerer, the convoluter, and the disingenuous than we are to people who are direct, almost immediately clear, and relatively unambiguous. (It would be unrealistic to believe that all issues can be discussed with absolute clarity and certainty.) The rarity of the articulate person is one reason why he or she is such a delight. Much more important is the fact that we generally know where articulate people stand, because they know how to tell us.

Articulate people often amaze us with their ability to think on their feet. Some years ago I developed an acronym that might help you sharpen your skills in thinking on the spot: KEY. The letter *K* stands for "key point." Identify the important issue and give it to people up front. I discourage the Agatha Christie approach, which is to keep people in suspense. The middle letter *E* stands for "elaboration" or "explanation supporting the key point." Finally, for those of us who remember the keys used to wind up toys before batteries became popular, the last letter *Y* stands for "winding up your argument with a close that wraps it all up."

Remembering KEY will help you to organize your material extemporaneously. But organization is only one explanation for the acceptability of the articulate person's comments. Another reason is that articulate people often communicate their perceptions rather than what they might consider to be objective reality. "This is the way I see it," they say, "and this is the way I feel about it." Thus, they don't foist their vision of reality on us. They present their views and feelings, and leave it to us to describe ours. They are experts in their perceptions and feelings, and they make it plain that you are expert about yours.

Successfully articulate people use plain language that is easy to organize. They tend to minimize their use of jargon and technical terms, making it easier for others to understand the points they are making without having to run to a dictionary—and without making listeners feel inadequate, a sure way to cut off the dialogue. They tend to speak in short declarative sentences that are easy to organize. And they use the active voice in their verbs a lot, rather than passive voice.

Through the years I have come to realize that articulateness is not necessarily equated with intelligence. But articulate people do appear more intelligent than most, whether the appearance represents reality or not.

4. They Are Sensitive. Sensitivity may seem a strange term to use with regard to power-track people. It seems at odds with those commonly identifiable traits considered desirable in management, especially competitiveness and aggressiveness.

Most people fit within one of the following three categories of sensitivity:

- *Sensitive* people operate as open systems, interacting in healthy ways with others. They are centered as opposed to self-centered and can respond to others without losing their sense of who and where they are. Just as they require psychological space, they respect that of others.

19

- *Insensitive* people are self-centered and can't concern themselves with others, even when those others can affect their career advancement and power building. They erect psychological barriers that protect them from the feedback of others. They do not permit anything to disturb their self-images.

- *Hypersensitive* people have inadequate boundaries to protect them from external influences. It is easy for them to lose their balance. They lack the toughness that is necessary for a realistic self-image.

Excessively self-centered and hypersensitive people have trouble staying on a power track. The former fail to see signs of change around them and are unaware of the negative feelings that others have toward them. Hypersensitive people see the changes but fail to analyze them before they react. Neither is sufficiently rooted in reality to know what is happening around and to them.

Successful persuaders are sensitive to what others might want and can contribute to an interaction. They are skillful at sensing the verbal and nonverbal language of others. The expert seeks to involve the other person in any transaction, knowing that the other has something to contribute—knowledge, experience, ideas, and resources, all of which can be helpful to the influencer. If you don't involve others in your transactions with them, there will be little or no communication and understanding—and no persuading.

Experienced persuaders are also sensitive to time and situation. There is a time and place for everything, and they are ever alert to how and when to go after certain kinds of actions, decisions, or requests.

5. Influential People Have Credibility. They have developed a reputation for dealing squarely. Without abandoning their own interests or letting down their own boundaries, they are careful not to ride roughshod over those of others. Persuading is not usually a matter of winning friends. To influence others, you do not have to be loved. But you must be respected and trusted. Undoubtedly we all know people who are amiable but who frequently promise more than they can deliver.

Credibility is probably the most important characteristic of the successful persuader. Real believability takes time to build, but, as many people have discovered to their profound regret, not very long to destroy.

Credibility has to do with others' trust in you. They must be confident that you will not knowingly deceive them. Making a mistake in fact or judgment is one thing—people forgive that— but being guilty of deception or falsifying, or promising and not delivering, are not usually forgivable. Such flaws shatter credibility beyond repair.

As I've indicated, credibility is much more important than likability. It is much more closely related to confidence, self-knowledge, and competence—to knowing rather accurately what you can do. In fact, some very credible and persuasive people may not be warm and genial. They may even be gruff and distant. But in working with them, you are aware that they will not ignore your interests in the transaction, especially if they have committed themselves to helping you realize your goals or to respecting your interests. At the very least, you know that in looking after their interests, they will not knowingly violate yours by deception.

6. Influential People Know How to Deal with Opposition. They are cool under fire. Many people get defensive in the face of disagreement. Good influencers don't, and thereby strengthen their positions. Others observe their calmness and quiet determination and can be convinced of the persuader's arguments or opinions. In other words, anyone so self-possessed must be right.

Good persuaders even welcome a certain amount of open opposition, because hidden opposition is very difficult to deal with. Also, resistance openly expressed can be tested and verified. If it is real and justified, then the persuader knows what he or she has to do to make the sale.

You can take some helpful hints from professional salespeople in dealing with resistance. For example:

- *Ignore it.* Most people not trained in selling find ignoring resistance to be very strange advice. But the fact is that initial objections to an idea or a project are not always real. A critic of your idea may seize upon the first objection that comes to mind. He or she has a deep-seated antipathy to the proposition, but it's not well thought out. So you'll hear a more superficial resistance through such comments as "I don't think they'd approve that," or, "We tried that, and it didn't work," or, "That's going to bust the budget." Don't train your artillery on ground fog.

Accept the resistance. You don't have to agree with it. Acknowledge that the other person feels that way, and remain positive. Emphasize some of the benefits of the proposal. If the same kind of resistance keeps coming up, then you'll have to confront it. Marshal your arguments in response. When you sidestep arguments, resisters are usually disarmed. They expect you to become defensive and disputatious. Instead, you relax, accept that they think that way, and sell some other benefit of the idea or project.

I train salespeople to think in terms of "Yes, and . . ." rather than "Yes, but . . ." The defensive person confronts the opposition with "Yes, you think that way, but here's why you are wrong." Such a reply discounts the objector. You've challenged him or her, and the fight is on. But when you say, "Yes, I can see that you believe that [the objection] is a consideration, and here's something else I'd like you to consider." You sidestep the objection. Relax, accept, and sell something else.

• *Make the resistance a group issue.* If other people are involved in the presentation and the decision, you shouldn't always assume that since the idea is yours you must be its sole defender. When you're part of a group, let someone else discuss the opposition before you do. Most other people will have more credibility, because, at least ostensibly, they don't own the idea. They're probably not identified as being as emotionally invested in it as you are. Time after time, I've had my ideas resisted in groups, remained silent, and had those ideas sold by others in the group.

Making the resistance a group issue is a risky thing. You have to know just how long to remain silent. But if you get help from others, a large part of the selling is done.

• *Keep the opposition out of the personal arena.* In a vibrant organization, conflict is inevitable. Expect it. Follow the salesperson's example in not allowing opposition to become personal, even if you suspect it is. Always confront issues, not personalities. If the opposition is obviously personal, others involved in the decision making will see it. If there is no one else involved except the objector, keep the discussion on the issues and stay as positive as you can be. In time, when you have failed to rise to the bait, the objector may give ground.

Finally, successful persuaders come prepared for a hard sell, if necessary. But they don't let their worst-case scenarios stand in the way of responsive communicating with an objector. Their responses to objections are not framed in "I win-you lose" terms but are rather designed to keep the door to communicating and persuading open.

7. Influential People Know How to Ask for Action—and They Do. Many people are afraid to come right out with what they want. The most common explanation for this reluctance is that they fear rejection. So you'll have a conversation with an associate who drops by your office and then leaves, while you wonder what the person wanted from you. Or you'll read a long memo with the suspicion that the writer wants you to do something, but you don't know what. A flagrant example of such obscurity was the manager who frequently wrote very reasoned, analytical memos for the management group of which he was a member. They were never discussed in their regular meetings, a fact that infuriated him. But, then, he never told his colleagues in his memos that he wanted them put on the agenda.

Yet, not asking for the action you want goes against psychological reality. A satisfying transaction has a beginning, a middle, and an end. Transactions that don't close are frustrating to the people involved.

Other people don't achieve closure because while they think they have, they really have not. Your boss comes to you, for instance, and says, "Don't you think it would be a good idea if we published a memo every week showing our output?" You, thinking the feedback would be good for motivation, readily agree. The boss nods and goes out of your office. Next week he asks where the memo is. He thought you understood he was asking you to do something. You thought the idea was cooking. People are forever saying things such as, "Does this make sense to you?"

or "Do you agree?" but making no call for specific action. Then they wonder why nothing happens.

Influencers realize that the output of their effort is more important than the input. The persuading isn't finished until someone does something. The desired end may be simply to get someone to accept an idea or an opinion. That's fine, if the other person knows that's what's expected and signals agreement. In other cases, it's an action that must be taken. Influencers make it very clear what action they want. You don't sit in the company of a good persuader and wonder very long about what he or she would like from you. Good persuaders understand how favorably they are regarded by others, who appreciate their clarity and forthrightness.

8. Influential People Know What Motivates Others. Remember, influencers are salespeople, and good salespeople know what motivates prospects to buy. The first factor in the buying decision is, Is this product good for me? Does it provide a benefit that I want or need? Will I be or feel rewarded by buying it? The second factor is, Can I obtain this benefit or reward without undue effort or risk? The salesperson talks about how what he or she sells will reward the prospect: It will save you 20 percent per month. It will provide more hospital benefits plus nursing home care. It will increase productivity by 40 percent.

But the reward must be attainable. Easy financing is available. We'll have it installed this week. We train your people; you don't have to worry.

These two factors, value and probability of success in attaining the reward, are central to motivation theory, which good influencers go with. When you want to sell a new program or policy, spell out the benefits, the pluses, and make it easy for management and your clients to enjoy them.

Remember these three recommendations. When you have an idea, proposal, or project,

- Make it interesting—otherwise no one will listen to you.

- Make it valuable—it must appeal to the self-interests of others.

- Make it easy—if it isn't seen as do-able, then it won't be done.

PRINCIPLES OF PERSUASION

At some point while, as a member of the professional staff of RIA, I was counseling managers on how to develop more effective behavior in themselves and others, I realized that my recommendations were based on selling principles I had used as a salesman. I recognized that I was treating the managers' interactions with others much as I'd view a sales transaction, with each party to it wanting his or her needs met by it. Out of this recognition came five persuasion principles to guide managers through their various transactions. Here they are in summary:

1. Know your product.
2. Know your prospect.
3. Involve your prospect.
4. Ask for action.
5. Be prepared to handle opposition.

Let's look at each of them in detail:

1. Know Your Product. What idea, project, solution, or opinion are you selling? Your product can be any of these, or it can be you. If you've ever asked for a raise or placed yourself on the list for promotion, you know what selling yourself can be. Is your product the training you can offer? No, it's more likely that your product is the effectiveness that the training will help bring about. In defining your product, think in terms of output, not input. What will happen as a result of your efforts or your programs?

Whatever you are selling, know what you have to offer. What are the strengths and the benefits? Why should others buy you or your ideas? You cannot reasonably hope to persuade anyone or anything until you have first been able to convince them that you know what you are talking about, that you are credible.

Just as you distinguish between input and output, know the difference between features and benefits. Features are characteristics of the product. Benefits are what the product will do to meet the prospect's needs and wants. For example, the convenience of the training, the comprehensiveness, the specificity of the content, the authority of the presenters, the inexpensiveness—all these are features. In selling training, you must show how all of these features will contribute to the increased effectiveness of the people being trained. When you suggest the results to the client, you are talking benefits—reduced costs of operation, faster response time, increased productivity, improved technical skills. Think of the bottom line. That's what your prospect is buying, not your design, your audiovisual aids, not the slickness of the presentation.

You should mention features and inputs. Those help the selling process. They make your product more attractive. But trainers, like the general population, get stalled at that point. Think like a salesperson, who is trained to answer the prospect's question, "How can what you sell help me to do a better job?" Couple that question with another: "*What* can your product do to help me be more effective?" Of course, you want to impress the prospect that your program is the efficient way to train people, but in the prospect's mind, the word "effectiveness" holds priority. Effectiveness means getting results. Being more effective is getting more results more often.

An important part of knowing your human resources product is being able to anticipate how those whom you are hoping to influence view it. You may be selling a new program, a procedure, or a policy, but chances are you'll be seen as part of the product. Therefore, develop a profile of yourself as your prospects see you. What has contributed to your credibility and authority? Why should they buy you? What successful products have you delivered in the past? What are your demonstrated strengths and relevant resources?

In summary, as a human resources person, you'll do a better selling job if you think of yourself as selling effectiveness. Your product helps to make the organization run more effectively. Running a program, or a department, is simply your input.

Through the years, in exercises in my workshops relating to persuasion skills, one truth has become quite obvious to me: Most people are more skilled at describing their products than they are at relating their products to their clients' needs and wants. Hence, the second persuasion principle.

2. Know Your Prospect. You have to know, or learn, something of the other person's needs and wants. That information is essential if you are to translate what you want into benefits that are attractive to your prospect. What parts of your proposition would interest him or her? Is this a good time for your prospect to hear what you have to say? If the budget is tight, the greatest program delivering the most fabulous results will be just a fantasy. Is the prospect's operation rushed and overworked? Then there may be no time for discussions such as training and development. Perhaps your prospect would be more receptive at another time.

There are a number of ways to get to know your prospect's needs. One is to know the operation in general. If the whole organization faces a particular challenge, then you can assume the parts of the whole are concerned about it as well. Another is to maintain contact, to have chats and informal sessions with the prospective client. Still another is to know the environment in which the organization operates. What's coming down the road that your clients need to prepare themselves for? Many trainers do diagnostic surveys and studies and maintain advisory committees to feed them the necessary information on needs and concerns.

The important thing is to avoid seeming arrogant by walking into a prospect's office and declaring, "I have decided that this is a good product that you should buy." A more friendly and potentially successful approach is to say, "Based on your concerns and to help you operate more effectively, to get more of the results you want, here is a program (or a procedure) that I believe can work for you. I'd like you to take a look at it."

What kind of presentation will work with a particular prospect? How detailed, for example, should you be? Some like to get deeply involved with every aspect. Others want broad strokes. Should you be formal or informal? Would this prospect be more impressed with technical descriptions and the language of the profession, or should you talk at street level? The answers to these questions should be part of your knowledge of the prospect.

Remember that persuasion doesn't occur strictly on a rational level, even if your product is a rational one. Your listener will respond to your presentation in a number of ways—rationally, emotionally, and intuitively—and it is essential to be able to anticipate these responses. Prospect A likes to see himself in the vanguard. He goes for the "be the first on your block" appeal. Prospect B, on the other hand, needs to know that what you recommend has been safely tried by three thousand others with little risk. Ms. C has an aversion to developmental kinds of programs.

She seeks in them an implied threat: You need this because you—
or your people—are not performing well. Manager D complains
that he has been disappointed so many times with programs, and
he is skeptical.

The list of prospect variables is almost infinite. If you have a
Ph.D, say, you'll find some clients who like the academic identification, who are eager to work with you. Others may be put off
by your advanced degree, so you know that you must underplay
your credentials.

In short, people have biases that you must take into consideration. Salespeople know that even sales made to engineers are
seldom made solely on the specifications of the products.

3. *Involve Your Prospect.* Communication, goes the cliché, flows
both ways. The prospect brings ideas, biases, strengths, experiences, knowledge, needs, and wants to the transaction. You need
to hear them if they will affect your getting what you want. Besides, you need to take the prospect's temperature: How warm is
he or she to what you are suggesting? You need feedback on how
well you are doing, how close you are coming to the target.

Salespeople ask questions to involve the prospect. They
know that prospects consider themselves to be experts on their
operations and love to show that expertise. You have to provide
the invitation. So, you might pose questions such as "I would
imagine that you're concerned about . . . Am I correct?" or, "Am
I right in assuming that one of your big needs now is . . . ?" or,
"Tell me a bit about some of the concerns on your mind."

Many of these probing questions should be asked before the
actual presentation. There are at least two reasons for this. One
is to get information that you can use later in the body of the
presentation. The second reason for asking the question is to relax
the prospect and to build rapport at the same time. Chances are
the prospect has been thinking or worrying about some aspect of
the operation, and you'd like to help him or her make a transition
from thinking about the details of the operation to what you have
to offer. You also want to establish yourself in the prospect's mind
as someone genuinely interested in finding solutions to his or her
problems and in developing better ways to do things.

As you talk your way through your presentation, you'll want
to ask more questions, for example, "Does what I'm saying make

sense to you?" or, "Am I correct in assuming that this could provide a benefit for you?" or, "It seemed to me when I was thinking about this that this program could be promising and advantageous for your people. Am I right?" The answers will help you to create a dialogue rather than a monologue. They will also tell you how effective your preparation is.

Another reason you want to get the other person actively involved in your presentation is that most people have trouble listening. They are simply not trained to listen well. They tend to hear only part of what you say, or what they wish to hear—which may be quite different from what you are saying. Through your questions and invitations to respond you can find out what others have heard. Furthermore, even people who listen well have limited attention spans. If you don't change pace, if you don't get their participation, their minds wander.

The ultimate involvement of the prospect involves talking his or her language and matching benefits to that person's needs. We in human resources have to watch the jargon and the psychobabble, for which we are unfortunately well known. We pay no greater compliment to the prospect than to use language that he or she is familiar and comfortable with and to talk about problems that are specific to the prospect.

4. Ask for Action. There's an old joke about the man who prays each week that God will let him win the lottery. After many months without winning, the man adds in desperation the plea, "Lord, give me a break. Let me win the lottery!" From heaven comes a booming voice: "Give me a break, Sam. Buy a ticket."

You won't win without buying a ticket. You usually won't get what you want without asking. Remember the second characteristic of the influential: They know they have a right to try to get what they want. But some people, including salespeople, are very hesitant about asking for what they want. Putting it more strongly, they dread the moment when they ask for the order. They're afraid they'll be rejected. Or they assume that the other person knows what is wanted without being told or asked.

Asking for action provides closure for both of you and may also relieve tension or uncertainty, since the other person in any prolonged transaction has already figured out that you want something—help, a recommendation, a favor, acceptance of a suggestion or a program, acceptance of you personally. Few things are more frustrating than a transaction that is open-ended.

Experienced salespeople build to a yes. They try not to spring the close on a prospect without some cultivation. They'll seek a series of agreements. To illustrate, they start off by getting agreement on their perception of the prospect's needs: "You'd probably like to get your absenteeism under 15 percent. Am I right?" or, "One answer would be to install job rotation so that your key posts are more likely to have uninterrupted coverage. Isn't that correct?" Then as they describe the solution they ask, "Does this make sense?" They may even ask for approval of various features of the solution: "I would imagine that one of the more desirable aspects of this design is that none of your staff would be away from the department more than one-half of a day, correct?" Any time the salesperson can ask a question and reasonably assume the answer will be in the positive, he or she will. After a series of yeses, the salesperson closes more confidently: "Since we seem to agree that this plan would provide a solution for you, why don't you give me the okay to set it up as we've discussed?"

The sales veteran also sells to a no. That is, the seller continues to sell until he or she gets a definite answer, even if it is a turndown. Less stouthearted people will fold early. The prospective client says, "I'm not sure we can fit this into the budget this quarter," or, "I need to think about this," or, "I want to talk this over," or whatever. Whether it's a stall or an objection, the inexperienced will accept it and leave. The tenacious influencer decides not to leave until there is more definite action.

5. Be Prepared to Handle Opposition. Any time one person tries to persuade another to accept a new idea or to favor a project, it's only realistic to anticipate some opposition. At least some hesitation. Few people listen attentively, surmount their fears and biases easily, and surrender to someone else's logic. Probably the other person is sitting there asking such questions as, Will this make me feel less secure? How will my status be affected? Will the change result in inconvenience? Will I wind up working harder? Will I lose face? Those are just a few of the anxiety factors that erect barriers to the acceptance of what you are selling.

The key phrase in point number five is "be prepared." You

may not have to deal with resistance. You may not wish to. One way to handle opposition is not to. If the issue you are working with is complex, you may want to use Kurt Lewin's force field analysis. Draw a line down the middle of a page. At the top, on the left put the word "drivers"; on the right, the word "restrainers." For each reason why you believe the prospective client will say yes, draw an arrow pointing toward the line in the middle. If the driver or benefit is weak or only moderately strong, draw a hollow shaft on the arrow. If the reason to assent is strong, fill in the shaft solidly with ink.

Do the same thing with the restrainers, or reasons to say no. Those that are weak or moderately strong get an arrow with a hollow shaft. Those that are strong deserve a solid shaft.

What you have is a pictorial description of the forces that push for a yes against those that support a no. What drivers can you increase or strengthen? These are benefits to the prospect. How can you make one or more of them even more attractive? Then look at the restrainers—to see how you can weaken one or more of them. For example, if you were proposing a training program that seems very expensive, you might suggest that during the first session you train one of the client's employees as a trainer who can conduct further sessions. On the driver side, you might suggest a redesign of the program that provides one or two more benefits or areas of instruction without adding to the time needed for the presentation.

Doing a force-field analysis is a good way to summarize benefits and objections, to assess the relative strengths, and to alter the force for and against.

When making a presentation, informal or formal, you'll want to know how much opposition you'll have to try to get out of way during the body of the presentation. To illustrate, you anticipate an objection that has to do with disrupting the work force to be trained by saying in the presentation, "To avoid a stoppage of the work flow, we're prepared to hold the sessions one hour before or one hour after the work day. They'll get overtime, true, but there'll be no interruption in the work flow."

You must be selective in heading off anticipated resistance. If you try to take care of everything you anticipate may come up, you'll sound very defensive—and you may wind up giving opponents ammunition they wouldn't have come up with on their own. Thus, select only objections or reservations that you are quite sure will surface. Hold off the rest until you've asked for action, and then see whether they are voiced.

As I said earlier, when dealing with an objection don't jump to answer it unless you're reasonably sure it is a genuine concern of the person who brought it up. The usual method is to accept the objection and sell some more benefits. Sell as long as you can. The longer you are there, the greater the chance that you'll get more information that will be helpful to you.

Unfortunately, many people tend to take opposition personally. They believe that it is directed against them as persons, not against their ideas. Their response is usually to get very defensive. And they lose control of the transaction. Even if part of the opposition is personal, opposition often indicates the need for more skillful persuading. It tells you what you must do. A positive way to look at opposition—the way salespeople look at it—is to recognize that the person who is fighting you is at least involved. Nothing is worse than a prospect who ignores you.

In addition to looking at resistance positively, as a sign of involvement, it will help you to have a formula for dealing with it, once you decide to. There are five steps: relax, accept, sell more benefits, qualify, and close.

- *Relax.* Physically show signs of relaxation. Sit back. Let your body go loose. You'll find your mind will function better when your body is not tensed.

- *Accept.* Use the "Yes, and . . ." approach: "I can see that you regard that as a problem. I'd like you to take a look at some other aspects." Sell more benefits. You don't have to respond to anything at just that moment.

- *Sell.* You may want to elaborate on points you've already made, or you may want to introduce some new thoughts, now that you've heard from the other person. When you've finished, ask for action again, just as if the prospect had not hesitated.

- *Qualify.* You've now heard for the second or third time the objection, "I don't know. We tried something like that before, and it was a failure." You're confident that you're hearing the real thing. Qualify the objection: "If I could show you how my plan will avoid the problems that you had before, and how it will work when the other did not, would you give me approval to go ahead?" This is your final test of how well you've done, and whether the objection is truly real. The prospect will probably say yes, unless he or she is playing games. Now confront the objection with all the arguments you can muster.

- *Close.* Don't forget to ask for action.

This formula is appropriate for any situation in which you're encountering resistance. If you're in a group, you might wish to modify it slightly in the hope of making your proposition and the resistance to it more of a group issue. When the objector voices hesitation or a problem with what you've presented, relax and accept it. But don't say anything at first. Someone else may answer for you. If no one says anything, sell benefits and ask for action. This time someone may speak up, either answering the original objection or repeating it. If it's a repetition, stay quiet for a minute. If nothing happens, you may wish to ask the group whether anyone else shares the objection. You may find that the group generally does not, which is ammunition for you. But if the problem is widespread, qualify it.

PLANNING YOUR PRESENTATION

To help you put together a presentation that will have maximum impact, use the following form or one similar to it to organize your thoughts and the benefits to the client, before you see your prospect.

PRESENTATION PLANNER

Name of prospective client: _____

Prospect's statement of needs and symptoms of observable problems:

_____

_____

_____

_____

_____

_____

_____

Your perceptions of prospect's needs (if different or in addition to):

_____

_____

_____

_____

_____

Benefits to offer to meet needs (greater to lesser):

1. _____

_____

2. _____

_____

3. _____

_____

4. _____

_____

5. _____

_____

Anticipated Resistance:

Objection or stall: _____

_____

_____

Your response: _____

_____

_____

Objection or stall: _____

_____

_____

Your response: _____

_____

_____

In using the "Presentation Planner," don't confine yourself strictly to the rational. For example, in the section "Your perceptions of prospect's needs," you'll want to enter what you suspect are his or her psychological needs. Is the prospect highly competitive and looking to you to help add to his or her glory? Is the prospect on a fast track, looking for breakthrough programs? Does the prospect need the approval of others, especially higher management? Is the prospect feeling insecure in his or her job? Should you provide assurance, opportunity, stroking?

How can you translate the program's benefits into responses to these non-logical as well as logical needs? Think about the language you could use to convey reassurance and a sense of security, or to congratulate the prospect on taking risks. How can you reinforce the other person's tendencies to move in the direction you want? "You and I realize, John, that no one is ever as effective in any situation as he or she would like to be. And a lot of people are content with that. What I sense from talking with you—and I think it's admirable—is that you seem always to be on the lookout for ways to be a bit more effective in your dealings with others."

Where do you suspect the resistance will come from? Once

again, go beyond what you believe will be the rational objections or reasons for stalls—next quarter is a better time, the budget is tight, my people are overloaded right now, I have to go slowly to prepare them for this. You might translate those objections as the fear of taking a risk, of the disapproval of bosses and subordinates for introducing this program, of spending the money without proportionate results, of giving up authority. What you know of the prospect that could be translated into emotion-engendered resistance should be entered in the section "Anticipated resistance."

ALERT TO HERE AND NOW

It's imperative that anyone in human resources be a good listener. Being a good listener helps you to stay alert to what is going on in any transaction you have with another. And maintaining awareness of what you want from, and what is happening in, a transaction is fundamental to successful persuasion. Years ago, in studying Gestalt therapy, which encourages alertness to the here and now, I developed the following four questions that are useful to help people in transactions stay on the track to their objectives. It's very easy, especially if you encounter resistance or sloppy thinking in the other person, to get defensive or side-tracked. Rehearse the following questions so that they spring to consciousness automatically when you are working to persuade another. Your staying in control of the discussion—that is, guiding it to a desired end—contributes greatly to your getting what you want.

1. What Do I Want from This Transaction? Do you want information, help, an agreement, some form of action, or a commitment? You will have a specific objective in mind in most cases, but you look for other results as well. For example, you want the satisfaction of presenting your story in a complete and honest manner and getting favorable results from that presentation. You want your communication to be clear and acceptable. You would like the other person to believe that you are pleasant and rewarding to work with. You would like to be admired and respected. Furthermore, you would like this transaction to be the beginning or the continuation of a long and mutually beneficial relationship between you and the other person.

2. What Do I Think the Other Person Would Like? Obviously your listener wants to spend time wisely and learn something from the conversation. The other person probably has a specific objective too. He or she would like to get a good deal or a solution to a problem. That can happen only if you provide the facts and the motivation to do business with you. The other person would like to feel that it is possible to rely on and trust you. And finally, the other person would like to feel that his or her professionalism, prestige, feeling of self-worth, and other needs have been enhanced by what is going on between you.

3. What Is Going on at This Moment? You should not be so preoccupied with what you are saying and doing that you lose sight of the clues that the other person is giving. Is he or she interested, absorbed, following you, thinking about what you are saying? Are you being as effective as you could be? Are you trying to relate to the listener? How can you get a reaction or some participation? Does the other person have knowledge, opinions, or experience that you should try to tap at this point? If you don't have some idea of what is going on with the other person during the discussion, and if you aren't reasonably sure of your effectiveness, then you are not in control of the situation. You could be going nowhere.

4. How Does What Is Going on between Us Help Us Both to Get What We Want? If you want to lead some kind of action, you must determine the effectiveness of what is happening now. How does it contribute to your both getting what you want? If you don't know that, the presentation or conversation could go off the track and never get back on. To be truly in control of the situation, you must be constantly aware that what is happening at any given moment either contributes to the desired course of action or steers you away from it.

When your objective is to influence others—their thinking, their decisions, their actions—you'll find it helpful to ask these questions of yourself, and to do so automatically. If you do not really define for yourself what you want from the transaction, then you will probably have to settle for whatever you get, and that may be what the other person wants from you, in which case, the seller becomes the buyer.

ASSERTIVENESS-RESPONSIVENESS

I want to conclude this section with a discussion of assertiveness techniques, for two reasons: One, I am convinced that we can all improve our chances to influence by knowing how to express our needs and wants in a manner acceptable to others, and two, I hope that you will see some value to recommending and delivering such assertiveness training to some of your clients.

Assertive behavior lies somewhere on the scale between the opposing extremes of aggressiveness and non-assertiveness. Neither of those extreme behaviors is ever appropriate for a professional in human resources. Aggressiveness involves putting others down, humiliating them, trampling on their dignity, and broadcasting the message that the only person who counts is the aggressor. Non-assertiveness is saying, in effect, "I don't count. Only others do." It gets you trampled.

I've sometimes seen trainers adopt aggressive behavior, but not often and not effectively. Aggressiveness is one way to ensure a short tenure. But too many trainers come perilously close to non-assertive behavior for my comfort, when they simply accept management's or clients' bidding without analysis and without performing as experts. Trainers in such roles and situations virtually surrender any chance to be influential or to perform in a leadership manner.

Valuable as it was, assertiveness training, popular in the 1970s, has lost much of its appeal. It was essentially a personal development and communicating technique. But it has, thanks to a consultant named Malcolm Shaw, additional dimensions. Shaw, who conducts many workshops for the American Management Association (AMA), has added a behavior mode, responsiveness, to assertiveness. Responsiveness involves being sensitive to the needs and wants of others—one of the characteristics of influentials, as you'll recall. Whereas assertiveness means placing emphasis primarily on yourself, and secondarily on others, responsiveness stresses others first, you second. Being responsive is essential to negotiating, selling, conversing, and managing.

There are four steps in assertiveness:

1. *What I see going on.* "You and I are having problems collaborating on a project," for example.
2. *How I feel about what I see going on.* "I'm unhappy and frustrated that you don't get your material to me on the agreed-upon date."
3. *The change I want.* "I would very much like for you to observe our deadlines."
4. *The benefits of the change to you.* "I can be more friendly with you and enthusiastic about working together, which would be a change for the better since now I'm tense and annoyed and show it with you."

Now watch what happens when I'm responsive to the other person:

1. *What you see going on.* "I agree I'm late, but you're frequently inaccessible when I need to consult with you about my part of the work."
2. *How you feel about what you see going on.* "Equally frustrated—and angry, too, now that I see you blame me for it all."
3. *The change you want.* "I'd like you to set some time aside for me to work with you."
4. *The benefits of the change to me.* "You get my work the way you want it—and on time."

If you put the two together, you have an assertiveness-responsiveness mode. Here's what I see. What do you see? Here's how I feel about it. How do you feel about it? Okay, we don't care for what we see. What's an alternative that we can both accept? There you have the grounds for negotiating and working through conflict.

What impresses me most about the assertiveness-responsiveness technique is the problem-solving attitude engendered in the trainee. Most people, I believe, look upon people with whom they have disagreements as adversaries. *"They're* out to block me," they think. *"They're* not interested in working with me. *They* don't see what they're doing wrong, and *they* don't care."

But they usually do care. They have their own perceptions

of the problem. They bring their own perspectives, experiences, strengths, and resources to the transaction, and all these can be helpful in finding a mutual solution. We sometimes find it hard to remember that those on the other side of a conflict are uncomfortable, too, that they have a point of view they regard as equally important, and that they are often quite willing to work toward a solution that meets their needs.

In workshops I often put the trainees through an exercise that calls for them to influence a co-worker who is showing resistance to a project. What the exercise often reveals is that most people know their products far better than they understand their prospects. When they encounter resistance, they are more likely to find new arguments as to why the prospects should buy, arguments based on the merits of the products rather than on the needs of the prospects.

When trainers do this with clients, the message likely to be perceived is one of arrogance: This product is good for you, regardless of your circumstances and needs. We need to remind ourselves that our most successful influencing occurs when we recognize that the selling situation is a transaction into which both parties enter freely and from which both wish to emerge with something that is important to them.

Regardless of how much power you can accumulate, your long-range effectiveness with others will always depend greatly on your abilities to persuade them that what you want will benefit them.

3

Building Your Base of Power

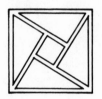

This statement is almost universally true: There is power in your organization that is available to you and that you are not using.

After thirty years in organizational life, I've been able to identify and define twelve sources or kinds of power that exist in virtually every kind of structure, even the most bureaucratic. Most of them have relevance to you, even though you might be in a staff position. In this section you'll have ample opportunity to examine each source or kind and to consider how you can best avail yourself of it.

I should make it clear at the outset that the twelve sources are not entirely separate. You'll quickly note that many of them, perhaps all, are interrelated. In some cases it may be that you cannot build one kind without having built another before. But even though they are not necessarily discrete, they are distinguishable.

Here then, briefly, are the twelve sources of power that you'll be reviewing in detail:

- *Competence.* Probably the cornerstone of any power base. Quite simply, competence means being good at what you do.

- *Personal.* The substance you project as a person that commands the respect of others.

- *Assigned/Delegated.* The authority (and responsibility) that is passed to you from above.

- *Associative.* Power that comes from your association with other powerful people or with being identified with them.

- *Resources.* What you have that others need and want.

- *Alliance.* Power deriving from allies within the organization who agree to join in a coalition with you.

- *Reward.* What you are able to give others that they value.

- *Professional.* You can earn credentials in your field and the respect of your peers, both of which impress your co-workers.

- *Availability.* Being in the right place at the right time.

- *Autocratic.* The power that flows from your being indisputably in control.

- *Charismatic/Visionary.* Your aura or vision that inspires people to follow you.

- *Position.* The power vested in your box on the organization chart.

Each of the above is described at length in the following pages. As you read about each different source, think in terms of how much you are already using it, how much more you could take advantage of it, or how you can begin to avail yourself of it if you are not doing so now.

COMPETENCE POWER

I'm confident that you cannot build a firm and enduring power base without being competent, without being able to deliver your product in a skillful and effective manner.

There are seeming exceptions to my premise, I realize. Years ago I encountered a phenomenon that I have since come to recognize is not uncommon. The vice-president of an insurance company hired a promising young man as his director of agencies, who would be working directly with the company branch managers or general agents. It was a key position, and the recruit—I'll call him Edward—seemed exceptionally qualified. He had been a successful agent in the field and had served as an assistant director in a large company. He was bright, personable, and knowledgeable.

Yet after a few months it was obvious that he had sold the company the only product he really had to offer: himself. He was incompetent. His relationships with the company general agents were marred by falsehoods, misunderstandings, and insensitivity. His boss didn't know what to do with him, but he wasn't fired. Finally, after a scandal involving the director and a female employee, the company terminated him.

A short time later, he turned up in an even more responsible position with more salary in a larger, better known insurance company. After perhaps two years there, he was handed a general agency in the field by that company, with an opportunity to make a great deal of money. However, after a few more years, he disappeared.

For several years this man had progressed from good to better, even though once in the job it became obvious he had nothing to offer. But no one responsible for hiring him wished to admit that a terrible mistake had been made. Each employer gave him good references. The last company he worked for, still not wanting to recognize their error, gave him a plum field assignment, in which he failed to deliver, as he always had.

Anyone who has been around organizational life has seen examples of Edward. For a time, they seem to go on to better things each time they move, but eventually they run into someone who says: "No further."

With Edward and all his facsimiles in mind, I repeat my premise that you cannot build a firm and *enduring* power base without competence. It is truly your cornerstone. Without competence, your base will eventually collapse.

What Competence Involves

Several years ago, ASTD developed a competency study, entitled "Models for Excellence," which identified thirty-one competencies important for excellent performance in the training and development field. As your eye runs down the list, you'll see that many of the competencies are in truth important for any position in the human resources field.

In the self-assessment quiz that follows, I've paraphrased some twenty of the competencies measured in the study.

SKILLS	YOUR LEVEL OF MASTERY		
	PROFICIENT	COULD USE IMPROVING	DEFICIENT
1. Understanding of how adults learn as opposed to how children learn.	☐	☐	☐
2. Identifying the skills required to perform jobs, tasks, and functions in the organization.	☐	☐	☐
3. Using a computer.	☐	☐	☐
4. Knowing the difference between objectives and activities.	☐	☐	☐
5. Writing clearly and effectively.	☐	☐	☐
6. Platform skills.	☐	☐	☐
7. Having a broad understanding of the key concepts, technologies, and practices in the training and development field.	☐	☐	☐

	YOUR LEVEL OF MASTERY		
SKILLS	PROFICIENT	COULD USE IMPROVING	DEFICIENT
8. Knowing how to facilitate the efforts of people in groups to achieve their objectives.	☐	☐	☐
9. Understanding and utilizing group process—the interactions of members of a group.	☐	☐	☐
10. Analyzing training approaches in terms of their relative cost-benefit ratios.	☐	☐	☐
11. Projecting trends and their possible implications for clients.	☐	☐	☐
12. Understanding the strategies, structure, power relationships, and financial status of your organization.	☐	☐	☐
13. Identifying organizational behavior theories and concepts in interactions and relationships on the work scene.	☐	☐	☐

47

	YOUR LEVEL OF MASTERY		
SKILLS	PROFICIENT	COULD USE IMPROVING	DEFICIENT
14. Using organizational behavior concepts and theories to influence behavior of clients and trainees.	☐	☐	☐
15. Understanding issues and practices in such human resources areas as job design, human resource planning, compensation and benefits, personnel research, employee assistance, and selection and staffing.	☐	☐	☐
16. Relating to people in different functions and at different levels in the organization.	☐	☐	☐
17. Having a general sense of the environment in which your organization operates—the industry or sector, economic or political impact, trends, and so forth.	☐	☐	☐
18. Thinking analytically and creatively: exploring and using a broad range			

YOUR LEVEL OF MASTERY

SKILLS	PROFICIENT	COULD USE IMPROVING	DEFICIENT
of ideas and practices and adapting theories to practice.	☐	☐	☐
19. Gathering information from various sources and doing research.	☐	☐	☐
20. Obtaining win-win agreements in decision-making situations.	☐	☐	☐

I'll briefly summarize some of the crucial areas of deficiencies I've noted in many of the human resources people I've known, especially in recent years.

- *Theory base.* Many people entering the human resources field don't have a theory base in human and organization behavior. They tend to learn programs and techniques without being able to determine whether these truly reflect the realities confirmed by research in the behavioral sciences. Without such discernment skills, these trainers are severely limited in their intellectual versatility and analytical abilities. At the very least, people entering the practices of organization behavior and development should be thoroughly familiar with the better-known writers and theorists, such as Fritz Roethlisberger, Warren Bennis, Alfred Marrow, Chris Argyris, Robert Blake and Jane Mouton, Rensis Likert, Abraham Maslow, Frederick Herzberg, Douglas McGregor, Warner Burke, and the others who have helped to shape our thinking over the past sixty years.

- *Adult learning.* Reading Robert Mager and Malcolm Knowles is obligatory. Many trainers, especially those who have come from education, use pedagogical approaches rather than those pertaining to adult learning. Adults have little tolerance for having their heads stuffed full of knowledge unless they see the value of that knowledge to them, especially as it relates to helping them be more effective in their work and careers.

- *Business awareness.* Again, many trainers come from the public sector with little knowledge of how other kinds of organizations, especially businesses, operate. They seem to regard themselves as citizens of a different country from the one their co-workers belong to, and they don't even try to bridge the gap. Unwittingly, they broadcast a message of arrogance to prospective clients: We're beyond having to know your problems and concerns. Not knowing intimately the business and the environment in which it must survive seriously cripples a trainer's ability to function effectively, to be at all influential.

- *Group process and facilitation.* What goes on between participants in a training group and between them (whether as individuals or a group) and the trainer can strongly affect the efficacy of the training. Yet many trainers have been insufficiently trained in this component of adult learning (the other two being content and methodology). When trainers do not have a firm grasp of group dynamics, they are relatively unprepared to deal with resistance, authority issues, conflict, and group building.

Of course, we have to bear in mind that all of the above competencies are inputs. They make a human resources professional efficient, but not necessarily effective. Effectiveness is related to results. The trainer who says "We've run six hundred people through our time-management programs" is talking about an input, or to put it less politely, "BOCs": butts on chairs. The more significant boast would be "After putting six hundred people through our time-management program, managers in those departments report an average increase in productivity of 22 percent. Both the managers and their subordinates report a cause-and-effect relationship. They were able to develop processing systems that reduced the time and people necessary to accomplish tasks."

Trainers often tend to get wrapped up in the inputs and in being efficient. They develop elaborate training designs, create imaginative and attractive visuals, schedule delivery realistically, and polish their platform skills. But all these are secondary to the consideration of what happens as a result of the training.

Your competence will in the final analysis rest on what you are able to accomplish for your client. Your product is effectiveness. The client wants more of something or a better something, when your training is complete. The client judges the accuracy of your diagnosis and analysis and the relevance of the training. In short, you are delivering the right thing and delivering it well, and does it work once you've delivered it?

Human resources professionals who are not on top of their field and who do not understand the problems, concerns, and needs of their clients will, it is safe to say, never score high on competence ratings. Consequently, those same people will always complain about their lack of power and influence.

PERSONAL POWER

Personal power is easier perhaps to recognize than to define. And you do recognize it. You can walk into a room of people and, after a few minutes, spot the people who project power. They carry themselves differently, speak differently, relate to those around them differently. For many years my office was located in a large building, occupied chiefly by a giant advertising agency. When groups of agency people got on the elevators, I had no problem identifying the power people by the way they walked and talked. My identification would quickly be verified by the deference the others showed toward them.

Personal power may have little or nothing to do with one's position. Several years ago, a friend of mine left a flourishing law practice to become an associate professor at a prestigious law school in the Midwest. After he had been there perhaps a year, I visited his office. As we walked down the corridor and rode the elevator, we met his academic colleagues and sometimes stopped to talk. Later, I remarked on the obvious respect for him that came across from the other professors. He discounted my observation. Yet, about a year later, he became dean of that law school. His peers had already sensed that he was a bit special.

Some people seem to have personal power from childhood, although most of us develop it later in life. When I was a boy in military school, I noticed that a few boys were natural leaders. When they became cadet officers, they were able to assert leadership over a bunch of unruly adolescents almost from the first day of their promotion. The rest of us officers never entirely succeeded in mastering our responsibilities. The natural leaders displayed a confidence that I thought was remarkable—and enviable—in boys of seventeen.

Indeed, confidence is a component of personal power. Competence is another. People who project personal power seem to have a strong sense of who they are and an equally strong belief that they are very good at what they do. Not incidentally, my law school friend had manifested both that sense and that belief in college, where I first knew him.

Who Are You?

You'll recall that influentials know they must have goals, and those goals provide a strong clue to who those influentials are. Your goals tell you a great deal about yourself. Simply having them is a significant indicator of confidence. Many people don't have clear objectives.

If you seek power, your goals should be clear and specific. And they should be moderately long-range. For example, what would you like to be doing in three to five years? It's rather difficult these days to project much beyond five years. The world is changing very fast, and opportunities appear and disappear rapidly. But you can plan for at least three years, and perhaps a bit longer. It is essential that you do so, to provide yourself with a sense of direction. Power people are not reactive. They are definitely not the we'll-see-what-happens type.

It's probably best not to have very many goals, no more than three to five. Any more than that and you lose track. You might be very comfortable with only one. The important consideration is that all goals have to be realistic. Do they reasonably reflect your abilities and potential? Are they truly what you want to do? Goals that are based on other people's assessments of what you should do are not as compelling as those derived from your own drives. Can you hope to achieve those goals without undue effort? If not, they are probably idealistic, not realistic.

Once you set your sights on specific goals, you can save yourself considerable anxiety and possibly some grief if you also establish secondary goals and alternate plans. Certainly you need subgoals, to let you know that you are on your path. Review your goals from time to time, at least once each year, to make sure you are going where you really want to go, given your growth, new interests, and changing conditions and environment.

Undoubtedly the most important aspect of planning your life is doing what you like to do, because there is a strong correlation between what you like to do and what you do best. So ask yourself these questions:

- What am I doing now that I would hate to have to give up?

- What am I doing now that I would like to do more of?

- What am I not doing now that I would like to do?

- What am I doing now that I don't want to be doing in three to five years?

How You See Yourself

Here is a three-step exercise that I recommend people use to develop a clearer profile of their strengths and resources, their weaknesses, and their main and fringe interests. It is also an exercise that can increase your self-confidence and feelings of worth, both essential contributors to your personal power.

Step One. You'll need pen and paper, or preferably a cassette. The idea of making your evaluation aloud may make you feel a bit self-conscious, but the one big advantage it has over doing it on paper is that you'll hear yourself as others hear you. You may wind up with a new insight into yourself and your resources.

Pick a time and place where you won't be interrupted. Then

imagine you are one of your co-workers. An executive search firm calls you to get more information on your associate (actually you). They ask you to be as candid as possible in assessing all pluses and minuses. Talk as if you were addressing the caller from the search firm. Review what your co-worker does well—and not so well; about what he or she likes—and doesn't. For example, discuss:

- Principal job functions and responsibilities.

- Functions and achievements in previous positions and skills acquired that might be useful to career progress.

- Tasks that your associate performs now and then that are not a primary responsibility but which tell one a great deal about the person's work habits and commitment.

- Functions he or she appears less suited to perform.

- Outside professional activities, such as membership in ASTD, that have broadened your associate's experience and expertise and that might be useful in another position.

- Any academic background that might contribute, such as a degree in organizational behavior or organization development (O.D.).

- The person's preferences. For example, does your associate prefer platform experience, program development, or instructional technology?

- Your colleague's career ambitions and goals, with comments on how strong the motivation is for each.

- The person's frustrations and failures.

- What characterizes his or her relationships with others on the work scene: warmth? professionalism? ease in establishing new relationships? frequent conflict and misunderstanding?

- Functions that your associate could perform better with training and development.

- What kind of an organization—large, small, public, private— the person prefers.

- What other associates like and dislike about this person.

- What you believe others respect and admire in this person.

- Functions that he or she does not like to perform.

Step Two. Now play back the tape and from it make a list of strengths and weaknesses, likes and dislikes. You're quite normal if your assessment wasn't totally candid. As you listen and make notes, it may occur to you that you played down a strength or played up a weakness. Underline it for emphasis. Or the opposite may be true: You spent a lot of time talking about a strength that on reflection doesn't seem all that impressive. Circle it for later, when you can think more about why you put so much emphasis on it.

When you've finished the list, you should realistically assume that you have favored your pluses and underplayed your minuses. Test yourself on this. Exaggerate each strength. To illustrate, you see yourself as time-conscious. Take that strength one step further. Is it possible that you are compulsive about time, the kind of person who can't stand being five minutes late and can't tolerate lateness in others? If you feel you relate well to others, including strangers, might you be so free and easy that others find you glib? You may be great at making acquaintances but less so in developing serious relationships, because others don't take you seriously. Or you see yourself as articulate and well-read—consider whether you show off your erudition with jargon, technical words, and uncommon words and expressions such as abound in the human resources field.

Look over each exaggeration. Some you can reject, others may be uncomfortably close to the truth.

Step Three. Put a plus next to each strength, such as communicating, supervising, planning, or relating, that others have confirmed in their feedback to you, whether they are colleagues, clients, or trainees. Then place minuses by the weaknesses that others have noticed. Now you have an element of objectivity in your self-appraisal.

Now that you've developed a list of areas in which you believe you have some qualifications and areas in which you are less skilled, perhaps the first thing you should do is be starkly realistic about the weaknesses: How important are they in your career? Decide as honestly as you can whether your lack of qualifications in certain areas will impede your progress. You want to build on strength. Taking time away from that to try to wipe out a weakness could be self-defeating.

Nor should you embark on a program to develop every strength. The time, energy, and money required to turn aptitudes into strengths have to be considered. Establish priorities, which will show you what you must concentrate on.

Chances are that your list of strengths will add to your self-esteem. You probably don't spend a lot of time thinking about just how good you are or can be. Take pleasure in yourself, your resources, your accomplishments. Your pleasure will show in your projection of increased confidence in yourself.

What to Take Seriously

Once you've established your worth—or at least upgraded your evaluation of yourself—you may have to resist the temptation to take yourself very seriously. Many trainers do, though I'm not sure why. It may well be compensatory behavior: Most people don't take trainers seriously, so trainers must. Or it may be that so many of us come from the field of education, where we became accustomed to enjoying power and authority because we stood before a class. Whatever the reason for trainers seeming to be so full of themselves, the phenomenon not only does not contribute to our building personal power, it inhibits the process. People who take themselves very seriously are often seen as pompous. They become objects of scorn and derision.

That is not to say that powerful people aren't serious. Many are very serious. But they follow Spencer Tracy's splendid advice to young actors: Take your work very seriously, and yourself not at all.

Not only do people who take themselves seriously set themselves up as targets for the humor of others, they often have problems relating to others. They interact with others as if they hold some sort of edge, as if they possess a superiority. And of course, the superior person is not interested in getting outside himself or herself to determine what the needs and wants of the other person are. Without understanding the prospect, there's little chance of a sale.

But as a trainer you cannot take your work too seriously. In fact, you must, if you expect others to take it seriously. Unfortunately, many trainers take the mechanics of their work seriously—the programming, the design, the delivery—when what should be regarded seriously is the output of their work: the increased effectiveness and competitiveness of the trainees entrusted to them. If you can deliver effectiveness, not just a training program, you will be taken very seriously. If you can diagnose the needs of your clients and develop a solution that works, you'll have no problem with your image.

Enhancing Your Impact

Feel free to use speech patterns, posture, and dress, to project your personal power image. Successful executives do—so should you.

Take dress. You don't have to follow the "dress for success" formula. Your clothes needn't be expensive, but they should be tasteful. When I was a young editor, I wanted to dress more casually than I had during the many years I was a salesman. So I began to come to work wearing turtlenecks, sports combinations, shirts with no ties. Fortunately, my mentor intervened and persuaded me that I was undercutting my image as a managing editor and an author of books on management. I went back to three-piece suits. Almost immediately, I detected a change in how many of my colleagues regarded me. Gone were the jokes about my way of dressing. I could sense that people were giving me more respect. And they were more comfortable with me, because the way I now dressed was congruent with my responsibility and my growing reputation.

A number of years later, I understood how wise my mentor was and how lucky it was for me that she intervened. I attended an award dinner at which a man well known in human resources was to be honored. The invitations said "dress optional." Many attendees did in fact wear black tie. But the recipient of the honor wore a sports jacket and slacks. Despite his reputation, the number of books he had written, and the fine work that he had pioneered, I had trouble taking the man seriously.

It's unfortunate that we judge people in part by externals— or as we used to say in philosophy, by the accidentals—but we tend to do just that.

Many people you work with will attend meetings without suit jackets but I don't recommend this. I always wore my jacket, and no one ever made fun of me or tried to belittle my formality. I always felt that wearing a jacket enhanced my image, and I continue to recommend it to trainers today.

How well do you communicate? I'm not talking so much about when you're in front of a group with a prepared presentation. How do you come across in conversation and in groups? Are you articulate, concise, to the point? I advise you to practice thinking on your feet. Many people don't do it well. I've sat through innumerable meetings in which people spoke in a disorganized, time-consuming manner. After a while, others tuned them out, even though what the speakers were trying to get across deserved attention. Here's a good rule of thumb: Try to capture the attention of your listeners in the first fifteen seconds. My experience is that you begin to lose people at that point if you have not hooked them with something interesting. Remember the KEY formula that I described in Chapter 2.

For some reason—and I'm not sure we know why—people who talk fast have more credibility than those who talk slowly. Perhaps it's because we assume that when people talk fast they are in command of the subject. If you are a slow talker, increase your speed to moderately fast. If you talk too quickly, people don't follow you, or you sound slick. Talk often, too. Pundits may maintain weighty silence for long periods of time, but many people don't know what to do with pundits. Of course, you must be careful to have something to contribute, to escape being labeled a windbag. One co-worker used to drive me crazy by solemnly repeating what others had said. In a very short time, no one paid attention to these reprises.

Keep your vocabulary simple. Most people will not appreciate your using words they don't understand. I've illustrated this for years in my business writing classes. In the middle of my presentation, I use an obscure word. Then I stop and ask the trainees about their reactions to the word. At first, their statements are cautious: They were bewildered, wished they had access to a dictionary, or were distracted by trying to figure out the meaning of the word. After a moment, though, they open up to admit that they resented my showing them up—"I thought you were a pompous ass"—and some were very angry with me. By using an esoteric word, I lost my audience.

If your voice is high-pitched, practice speaking in a lower register. The more body to your voice, the greater the likelihood that others will want to listen to you and will take what you say seriously.

Writing as You Speak

Nothing conveys confidence and competence more than a natural and interesting writing style. The most natural style resembles your speaking style. So few people are skilled at good writing that the proficient stand out from all others.

Through the years you have developed an effective speaking style, chiefly because you get instant feedback. When you say something that puzzles or angers or delights, you can see it on the other's face. The feedback tells you that you need to modify your words, to elaborate, to keep on with what you are saying, or to apologize.

But when you write, you may not get fast feedback, or any at all. You don't develop a style that is natural to you. Instead, you are likely to adopt a writing manner that duplicates what you have read or been taught, or the style of a boss or mentor. Since most people are not effective in their writing, chances are you are not either.

When you write like you speak, you will be read more carefully. People will feel as if they are hearing you talk, as if they are with you. Your approach will be natural and easy to understand, unless, of course, you are ineffective when you converse.

Most people's writing suffers from poor organization, too many words, too much repetition, and an artificiality that gives little clue to the personality of the writer. It's what I call the "writing mode." If I were to ask you to explain something to me face-to-face, you would, if you knew the subject, probably be clear and effective. But if I asked you to put the same explanation into writing, you would probably not be nearly as effective.

I advise you to work on narrowing the gap between how you talk and how you write. It's not easy. You might begin with a good business-writing course. Try to find one that lasts at least three days. It generally takes that long to see what you are not doing well and to absorb—and accept—what you should be doing instead. From that point on, you just work constantly to apply the principles you learned in the course.

I cannot hope in this section to substitute it for a good program in which you are writing and receiving feedback on it. But here are some practical tips to help you move closer to a natural style on paper:

- *Get your main point down first.* Remember that people don't like to be puzzled. Their first subconscious question is, Why should I read this? Answer the question fast or you will lose your readers. (They won't throw your memo, letter, or report away; they'll simply put it aside for "later.")

- *Use common words and short sentences and paragraphs.* How short is short? I offer no absolutes, but a good sentence length is eight to fourteen words. Paragraphs of more than eight to ten lines are intimidating. You want to make your writing inviting. Most people won't work at reading you, and if they have to organize your material for you, they may give up.

- *Read aloud what you have written.* If you have a cassette player, record yourself, then listen to the playback. Does the style sound like you, as you might say it? When I write, I often find myself talking to my typewriter. It helps.

- *Delay sending important material.* Another way to reduce the artificiality in your writing is to compose your memo, letter, or report, then put it away in your desk drawer for a day or two. When you take it out, you'll read it with a fresh eye. You'll see all sorts of problems, ambiguities, and awkward phrases that you didn't notice when you first wrote it.

As your writing gets clearer and more effective, you'll notice that others' writing is plagued with poor organization, sentences that are convoluted and run on forever, uncertain objectives and purposes, and such stilted construction that you might think a computer had composed it.

Improving your writing skills will not only get you the responses and results you want, but a more powerful image as well. You'll stand out as one who expresses himself or herself confidently and competently. Chances are good that you will be asked to do writing for others, and that increases your impact and recognition.

One important caveat regarding your writing: Try never to put anything negative in writing. You may disagree with someone. You may wish to criticize someone. You may have to impose a tough policy. Avoid writing it down. The negative impact of words increases when they are put on paper. And they are permanent. Anything I ever wrote that was negative eventually came back to haunt me in the form of retribution. Granted, you may have to write down something negative now and then, but try to couch the message in positive terms. For example, instead of saying "You must stop doing this," say instead what the person or group should start doing. In short, when possible, deliver negative communications verbally, face-to-face.

Creating Visibility

My theory has always been that you can enhance the projection of your personal power image by making yourself more visible in the organization. It's important for others to know you exist. If everyone knows you, talks about you, refers to you, perhaps even quotes you, then people suspect that for some reason you are worth knowing and that you must be important. Therefore, achieve some celebrity for yourself. Effective, clear speaking and writing are two very good ways to make yourself more visible. I have three more recommendations:

1. Ask for What You Want. Remember that influentials know they have a right to ask for what they want. Exercise that right. No, you won't get everything you want, but you'll establish yourself as someone who knows his or her worth. When I was a young editor, I was hired at a low "probationary" salary. Four months later, I walked into my boss's office and asked: "Have I proved myself?" He said that I had, so I asked for a large increase. He was shocked, and said, "We don't give increases like that." I said, "That's what I think I'm worth." I got it. Five months later, I asked for another increase. I got some of that, too. And another, until I got my salary base up to where I thought it reflected my contribution to the corporation.

These days it's not quite that easy to get much money. But think of other status indicators. I know a trainer who likes to read the *Wall Street Journal* but is reluctant to ask for her own subscription. She reads others'. I think she is wrong not to ask for her own *Journal*. She may not get it, but she might get on a regular routing. Besides, she would broadcast a clear message: I'm worth this to you.

What do you want? Better furniture, time off to work at home occasionally, new equipment? No one is going to speak up for your value to the organization as fervently as you. Even if you don't get what you want, you establish a presence. You've said, "I don't intend to be ignored." Furthermore, when people see how much you value yourself, they begin to look at your contributions. They then begin to value you.

It helps if, when you ask for perks and privileges, you prepare yourself with reasons why it will benefit your manager or your organization to give you what you want: more knowledge and skills, more productivity, time saved, or whatever. This could be a selling job, so be prepared. Knowing what you want is not enough. Knowing why they should let you have it helps immensely.

2. Send Ideas up the Line. Make yourself more visible by suggesting changes, solutions, and innovations not only for your part of the organization but for the whole organization as well. Of course, you have to know the operation's needs and potential. Remember, the second persuasion principle is "Know your prospect." When you know the needs and wants of the organization, you can be more convincing and authoritative in suggesting solutions or benefits.

To help you shape your idea and make it salable, take these steps:

- Define the problems the idea will solve.

- Define the opportunities the idea will create.

- List the trade-offs the idea will create.

Once you've developed your sales presentation, decide on your best channel. Who are the influential people the proposal must reach? Who is the first person to contact? Which people can be counted on for support, and what is the best way to enlist their aid?

In selling, which is what you do when you present an idea, much emphasis is placed on getting to the right person, the one who has the authority to buy. Generally, you would go through your boss, not over his or her head. Don't waste your time giving presentations to people without authority unless they can help you make the sale, or unless they can at least lend support. If such people have influence with the decision maker, sell them just as hard as you will him or her.

Your boss will probably be your best adviser on how to present your idea. Don't rely on paper presentations unless that's the only way you can go. You're far better off petitioning the decision maker to let you give a verbal presentation, at least at first. You can always follow that up with writing.

The more your ideas affect the total organization, or its parts beyond the training function, the more clearly you establish yourself as helping to run the organization's business rather than just its training department.

3. Take on Extra Work. Volunteer or be receptive to taking on tasks and responsibilities that, strictly speaking, you don't have to. There are innumerable benefits to you from venturing outside your job description. First, you get a reputation as someone deeply committed to the welfare of the organization. Second, you gain visibility as you build your network of associates in the organization. Third, you get to know more about the organization and acquire new skills and knowledge. Taking on extra work can add several kinds of power blocks to your base: competence, alliance, associative, availability, and resources.

Creating a Presence

Personally powerful people are often described as creating a presence. When they enter a room, people look up. They seem to fill a lot of space. In a group, others often look to them for leadership.

Presence is undoubtedly a combination of several things:

carriage, physical appearance, and more subtle characteristics that project both competence and confidence. Presence also results from the attribution by others of authority and credibility.

Unlike charisma, presence can be developed. This entire section on personal power contains many recommendations that can help. It certainly helps to have a strong sense of identity: You know who you are and where you're going. It's also valuable to know what you are doing and to have a clear measurement of what you have done and can do. You need to be able to articulate what you know and to persuade others to accept you and your views.

ASSIGNED/DELEGATED POWER

People who are fortunate sometimes get asked to assume authority and responsibility that do not normally reside at their levels in the organization. The power that goes with the authority and responsibility has been granted from above.

Some people make their luck. They look for ways to pull down responsibility from above.

As a young editor with RIA, in fact the most recently hired, I was given a job that no one else in my department would touch. Each week I would contribute an article to a newsletter for managers that was a joint project with another department. Our department was responsible for sales management and marketing material, while the other wrote general management articles. It was a terrible publication, and no one likes to be associated with a loser. But in my naïveté, I assumed that eventually management would wake up to the fact that it was poor and would want to do something about it. After a time it became painfully obvious that the editor of the newsletter didn't know what he was doing. I found myself working directly with the other department head. My boss gave subtle suggestions that I should withdraw, but I kept thinking: Here is a publication that no one really wants. This may be my only chance for the near future to wind up with my own publication. So I kept working away at it, meeting my deadlines even though there wasn't much satisfaction in it.

Eventually management did take action, and since no one really wanted the job and I was familiar with the faltering publication, management "awarded" the job to me. It was fantastic. I had my own publication, and I enjoyed a great deal of editorial freedom. That publication ultimately became one of the most profitable products RIA had on the market. Every year, millions of mail solicitations for subscriptions went all over the United States. It was, to put it mildly, a heady experience. The gamble had paid off for me.

I use the story to impress on people who want to get on the power track that they should not only be willing to take on work that perhaps strictly speaking they could avoid, but that they should look for such opportunities. And sometimes jobs that are unpopular, that others consider to be real pains, turn out to be bonanzas. In another RIA example, a young editor returned from a vacation in Europe to find that she was being considered as chair for the next editorial conference. Plainly, this was a task that the senior editors were happy to avoid. In addition to meeting her regular workload, she would have to form a committee, negotiate with a hotel, coordinate committee plans for food, entertainment, and meetings, and arrange schedules and agendas.

She took the dirty job, and she and her committee ran a highly successful conference. She achieved visibility in the company. Everyone now knew her well. Her value in the eyes of the other professionals went up several notches. Talk about making lemonade when you have lemons . . .

Don't be hesitant, therefore, to volunteer or let people know you're available for work outside your usual responsibilities. The more you know about the operation, the more people within the organization you have a working relationship with, the more valuable an asset you'll become. And as people see you acquitting yourself well of the increased responsibility, you'll find that their esteem for you and confidence in you will rise markedly. So will your influence with others. And with influence comes power.

Of course, you must exercise judgment so that you do not become a patsy. When people see you as a dumping ground for all the jobs they don't want to do, they won't see you as a person to be respected. Sometimes a task constitutes a no-win situation: Everyone is actually in some way opposed to its successful achievement, but no one wants to admit it. So you get stuck with it, along with everyone's hope that you'll botch it. Then no one will have to worry—except you.

A Crucial Subordinate

Eugene E. Jennings, well-known consultant and author of *The Mobile Manager* (McGraw-Hill, 1971), has long advocated that the ambitious, upwardly-mobile person should become a crucial subordinate to his or her boss. The ideal boss-subordinate relationship involves one helping the other: You as a subordinate make your boss look good through your supportive performance, and the boss gives you a chance to grow and progress. And as a crucial subordinate it's great to hear the boss say, "What we've accomplished together is better than what I could've done alone."

You may be fortunate enough to have a boss who is willing to let go of more and more responsibilities, because your manager is working on his or her boss to the same ends. You may also have a boss who is willing to let you do more high-level work because he or she is happier doing less and less. That's great for you, because the more authority you acquire, the more power you pull down for yourself. And you build your competence power at the same time.

But you may also suffer a boss who is reluctant to let go of authority and responsibility, perhaps through personal insecurity or because you are perceived as a threat. So you have to be somewhat discreet about going after more power for yourself.

One key to getting more of the action is to find ways to do things your boss does not do well or does not like to do. You might call such duties your "dirty work list." Here are some possibilities:

- *Talking to people your boss doesn't like talking to.* They may be other managers, employees of other managers, clients, or even certain subordinates. If you hear your boss groaning about having to call so-and-so, suggest casually that you would be happy to make the call. Or ask, "Since you seem to be tied up, would you like me to talk with him?"

- *Getting information.* Your manager may have difficulty getting information that can't be obtained through formal channels. Or there might be a situation in which your boss cannot afford to let it be known that he or she is trying to dig up some facts. You have a network. You may be better at using the grapevine or at sleuthing than the boss.

- *Supplying skills your boss lacks.* Your boss may come to rely on you for ideas and suggestions about subject areas that he or she is not well informed in. Or the boss is great at developing programs but hates stand-up work. Or he or she can articulate wonderful ideas face-to-face but sounds dim-witted when trying to put it all on paper.

- *Covering for your boss.* Supplying the skills that your boss lacks may be a form of covering. Perhaps a better term is complementing. But there may be times when the boss is preoccupied by extra-departmental matters, and you offer temporarily to take over some of the boss's regular duties. Or your manager is distracted by personal problems, such as illness in the family or a child who is causing serious problems. These problems can take the boss away from the office or reduce his or her effectiveness while there. Fill in.

Should you be eager to cover for a boss who is an alcoholic, on drugs, goofing off, or is trying to conceal a serious medical problem? Any of these situations presents an opportunity for you to build your power as you take over more and more of the boss's functions (and others will know that fact even though you don't broadcast it). But there are dangers. For example, your boss may later turn on you if he or she resents your having been of help during the problem period. And if the boss gets caught, you may be tarred by management with the same brush. If the cover-up requires lying on your part, forget it. At some point, when the truth is out, you'll lose credibility, and there is little or no power without credibility.

Here's a checklist of possible areas in which you may fruitfully search for tasks and responsibilities that your boss may be willing to let you take over, at least temporarily:

- Is the boss taking work home regularly, and can you lighten the load by suggesting delegation of some of those burdens?

- Are there tasks that the boss took upward at promotion because he or she believed there was no one capable of doing them? Perhaps you are now.

- Which of the boss's tasks have become so routinized that others, especially you, could do them? The boss may now be bored by them, but they would represent a challenge for you.

- Are there tasks that the boss used to like to do but no longer does?

- Is the boss giving special attention to the work of one of your colleagues and thereby having to neglect some of his or her own work?

- Have you acquired skill and knowledge that you did not have formerly and that now qualifies you to take on some responsibility the boss has been holding back on because you were not up to it?

- Has the boss hesitated to delegate to you because he or she thought you were too busy? Perhaps you could explain that you do now have time.

- Are you performing tasks that you should delegate to your subordinates, to make time for duties your boss would like to pass on to you?

An important caveat regarding your taking on tasks and responsibilities that your boss has delegated: Keep the boss as informed as he or she would like to be. When a manager delegates, there is bound to be some anxiety that the job won't be done, or done right, or done the way he or she wants. If you take the work on, maintain close contact with the boss. Give your manager feedback on what you are doing and how you are doing it, until he or she is reassured. The more the boss feels reassured, the more reinforced he or she is in the notion that the delegation was a right move.

Selling Your Ideas

An important way to build assigned/delegated power is to initiate projects or programs that you can then be responsible for. Usually, of course, you don't have the authority to start something significant without the approval of your boss or higher-ups. Getting the boss to say yes might be relatively easy, depending on your working relationship with him or her. But when the idea or proposal has to go up the line, then you have to take more deliberate and perhaps cautious steps. Consider the following:

- *What is the best way to present the idea for a decision?* Sometimes the informal approach is more desirable. You sit down with the boss, talk it over, get a positive reaction, and receive advice on how to push it further. It may well be that your promotional efforts will continue to be informal, consisting of conversations with key people. On the other hand, some organizations seem to prefer a formal approach: You must write a report or a proposal.

- *Try for a presentation.* You'll want to give it yourself. Your argument with your boss is "Look, I know the ins and outs of the idea. It will save you the time you'll need to acquaint yourself with it. Also, there'll be questions, and I can answer them on the spot."

The presentation may be before your boss's boss, or with a group of decision makers. No matter how informal the atmosphere, remember your selling principles: Know your product; know your prospects; involve them; ask for action; be prepared to handle resistance.

It may be that your boss is reluctant to let you give the presentation. If so, ask that you be present as a resource during his or her presentation.

I advocate your trying to set up a presentation even though you must first submit a proposal, memo, or report. When you send a piece of paper up the line, you don't have much control over it, or over what happens when people read it. It needs to be shepherded. If you can't arrange for a presentation, get your boss's permission to talk one-on-one with the key decision-makers, to make sure they understand the idea and get their questions answered.

A few observations about your memo or proposal. Remember to make your key point first, so as to answer the question, Why should I read this? What does he (or she) want me to do? Some people try to set the stage with historical or analytical background before they make it clear what they want. Such procrastination usually creates resentment. People suspect that they are being manipulated. It's best to be up front and clear: Here's the problem and here's the solution for it. Here's why I believe it will work. And here's how we can put it into practice.

Caution: Being prepared to handle opposition is not the same as handling it. You don't want to put objections or fears into people's minds that may not already be there. Thus, avoid building arguments in response to an objection into the report, unless you are reasonably sure that the objection will be voiced.

However, if you have only one shot at presenting your ideas, through your report or proposal, then you'll want to consider including everything and hoping to impress your unseen decision makers with your thoroughness.

Looking for Problems

An under-utilized tool for pulling down power from above is the task force, a temporary problem solving, semi-autonomous group that usually deals with interdepartmental or interfunctional issues. Because the problems addressed don't fall within the jurisdiction of a single line of authority, the authority for the task force comes from much higher up. And the higher the source for the authority, the more power and prestige task force members enjoy.

Look for problems, therefore, that are shared by two or more functions, departments, or disciplines. Almost any such issue can be nutritious fare for a group solution, whether it is training, marketing, organizational structure, or technology. Often, the problems you're looking for will have been around for a long time, but no one wanted to take the initiative to tackle them, or knew how to do so.

So that you are not perceived as an interfering busybody, line up some support for the idea among the people who have experienced the problem or who will be most affected by the solution to it.

Since task forces are often involved not only with coming up with the solution to the problem but with its implementation, you may find yourself with some operating responsibility, something you wouldn't have had if you had simply stayed inside the training room.

ASSOCIATIVE POWER

Paul Simmons (name changed) was asked by his company to stage a multi-media presentation at an industry association convention. One member of the audience was a vice-president of marketing of a well-known corporation, who introduced himself to Paul after the show, handed Paul his card, and said, "If you're ever in my town, give me a call. We can have lunch."

Not long after, Paul was in the vice-president's town. Soon, Paul was in his company as well. Paul came in at a high level and from the outset enjoyed exceptional power and influence as the older man's protégé. When the vice-president was promoted to president, Paul's influence became wider and more substantial. He enjoyed associative power.

You can see Pauls in almost any type of organization. Some of them are quite content to bask in the association without worrying about building any special competence. Others realize that associative power can be precarious and add a number of other power blocks to their base. The first example I saw of this was as a young man entering the business world. The sales manager in charge of group insurance sales in the large insurance company in which I was a trainee had a sponsor/mentor in one of the veteran vice-presidents. But the sales manager was bright and ambitious, and while he benefited from the senior man's counsel and wisdom, he worked hard to build power on his own. When suddenly the older man was kicked upstairs to the relatively powerless position of senior vice-president, the sales manager was able to survive largely because of his competence.

His experience taught me an important lesson: Associative power is nice to have and can be remarkably effective in building influence, but it should be combined with other kinds of power. Later I was to learn a corollary of the above truth: Draw your associative power from more than one source, if possible.

Getting Outside Your Department

In most cases you're well advised to look for your power centers elsewhere in your organization, since most human resources departments are not power centers. In some rare situations you may report to an executive who is powerful, although most executives in human resources are not. But your boss may have the ear of the COO or CEO, or you may be able to build your influence to the point where you have their attention. With such a direct line to the top, you can enjoy the prestige of association.

Most human resources people will not be so lucky as to have the equivalent of the red phone on the desk. If you're in the majority, you'll have to go looking for your centers of power and for the organizational influentials. The most likely place to look is in the line functions, as opposed to the staff.

Once you have identified your targets, how do you make contact? The most obvious way is to become visible to them. And the easiest way is to learn and use people's names. One of the first things a salesman hears is this advice: Use people's names, because there is no sound sweeter to them. I'm astonished at the number of people who do not seem to understand this truth. People I have known for years in ASTD continue to say only "Hi" to me, when I know that they know my name. The practice breeds resentment. In contrast, I often tell the story of Barbara N. Barbara came to work at RIA as an administrative assistant. Within a few weeks, she knew almost everyone's name and used the name when she passed the person in the hallway. A short time later, nearly everyone knew Barbara's name. It was impossible to ignore the warmth and the interest she showed toward others.

Introduce yourself. Many of your co-workers will wait for someone else to do the introducing. Get used to working the hallways, the cafeteria, and the conference rooms. When you see someone you haven't met and who you know is influential, stick out your hand and say, "I've been wanting to meet you. I'm Terry Phillips and I'm the new management training specialist. I report to (or work with) Harry Wade."

Ask to meet with the influentials. They'll understand that you're eager to learn about the organization, and they'll respect you for it. Make it clear that you are looking for their perspectives on the organization and tapping their own experience, otherwise they may try to push you off onto assistants. Suggest having lunch or breakfast together. You may have to be patient and persistent. But in time, most people you pursue will eventually make space for you.

You may be able to tie your requests for time to specific

events. For example, the marketing department has achieved a triumph in gaining a 12 percent market share for a new product that is only eighteen months old. You can let the marketing vice-president know that you'd like his account of what went into such a successful effort. You can polish apples without being too obvious.

What do you have to offer a mentor or sponsor? Why should the person invest time and energy in you? Initially your potential sponsor or mentor will respond to your interest in and obvious respect for him or her and will probably feel an obligation to respond to your requests for help in getting to know the operation. From that point on, there is usually a *quid pro quo*. Some mentors like their coaching roles, especially if the protégés follow their advice. Sponsors will want to be identified with people they mark as comers. The better you become, the higher you advance, the more satisfaction and prestige they enjoy. You may enjoy their confidence, since you aren't threatening them. They may feel freer to talk with you about organizational matters that they wouldn't discuss with peers.

But you must be prepared to offer them something—perhaps your knowledge of the human resources field. What services or programs would they be interested in? You can describe and offer them. Think of the discussions as informational rather than influencing. You may have information about some aspects of the operation that you feel comfortable in sharing with them. A mentor or a sponsor usually is the type of person who likes to be in the know. How much gossip you can pass on depends greatly on your relationship and how much trust there is between you. Some people disdain gossip and say they don't indulge in it. But I have never shared that dislike. Gossip is one of the fascinating aspects of organizational life, and most people enjoy it.

The more proficient you are in your profession, the more knowledgeable you become about the organization and its operation, the greater are the benefits you have to offer a sponsor or mentor. Protégés, it seems to me, must work to achieve equality. They may never actually achieve it totally, but dependence in a relationship is something you strive to work out of. In so doing, you become more valuable in the relationship.

As you progress, becoming more knowledgeable and experienced, you'll find that your relationship with a particular mentor or sponsor will mature, and you'll want to move on. That alone is a good reason why you'll want to cultivate relationships with several influentials. When it comes time for you to move on, you'll have other influential people to turn to. And as I've indicated, it can be risky to invest yourself totally in a mentor relationship with one person. You must always consider the possibility that your mentor may move on to better things, leaving you behind. Or, as in the case I described earlier, he or she may be shunted aside or kicked upstairs; once out of the main traffic pattern, a mentor's or sponsor's value to you is limited. Furthermore, there may be disadvantages to you from being associated with a now powerless person.

Looking for the Power Centers

In your search for associative power, you start by looking for the power centers in your organization. Get to know the people on the power track. Seek to perform training and consulting services for them. Ask them to join your advisory board. Be seen in their company. Ask for their inputs on your human resources programs, informally. Find your mentor or sponsor from among them. Ask them to help you give presentations to management on your programs. Ask for their endorsement when you propose a project or a program.

Where are you most likely to find the power people with whom you'd like to associate? Some questions to help you start your search:

- *What departments, divisions, or functions get the most attention?* What group is the subject of frequent mention in the house organ, or of praise in the annual report? What group seems to receive a larger share of resources—money, people, space, equipment?

- *What functions have been growing faster than others?* This will clue you in on where the organization is putting its dollars and energies. Look for new facilities and for unusual mobility of people connected with them, which might indicate continual expansion.

- *Where have the promotions exceeded the normal or average rate?*

When new titles proliferate, it's a sign of vitality and expansion.

- *Who suffers least during cutbacks?* From time to time, almost every organization experiences reductions in its workforce, but favored or growth departments are often pared less than others.

- *Where have the top executives traditionally come from?* If you can identify the track that many of them have followed, you'll probably discover what functions of the organizations are most favored—marketing, finance, actuarial, systems, or others. Remember, though, priorities and values change. Study the past, but mix in your knowledge of what is going on now. Things may be changing.

- *What is the relative location of the divisions or departments?* Growth and favored functions are often in more desirably located, newer facilities. Within the home office, they will usually be more prominent in space, size, and location. They frequently get preference when new and more desirable space becomes available.

- *Which part of the operation has esprit de corps?* People who sense that they are part of a power group show greater enthusiasm, competitive spirit, even, unfortunately, arrogance. They talk and act like winners.

Of course, you have to combine the above information with what you can glean from the organization's strategic plan. Your analysis may reinforce the conclusions you've come to, or cancel them out.

Looking for the Power People

There are key individuals in your organization who have greater power than others, and many of them will be located in the power centers you've identified. The following are some key indicators that should help you spot these powerful individuals:

- *Impressive office decor or location.* Corner offices with fashionable furnishings and expensive equipment bespeak power.

- *Enjoy the company of top management.* Who frequently confers with the top brass? Who sits close to the influentials at meetings? They may share some of the power.

- *Frequently mentioned.* Listen for the names that keep popping up in memos and conversation. Frequent mention usually points to *wunderkinds*.

- *Member of power cluster.* Look at the context in which some people in the organization operate. They have strong, talented people as subordinates forming power clusters.

- *Sought after.* When you're at meetings or a company party, watch to see who is sought out by others. A manager walks into the room and is immediately approached or surrounded by others. No standing quietly and meekly in a corner for that person.
  Sometimes peers will seek the cooperation or at least the endorsement of another. This is their tacit admission that he or she is perceived as more powerful and influential.

- *Introduced with fanfare.* Sometimes power centers are brought in virtually intact from outside. Watch for the person who is introduced with much fuss and who, during the breaking-in period, retains the respect of others. Often someone who comes in with a big flash just fizzles or is subsequently ignored, but a new person who shows staying power is worth noting.

- *Significant upward progress.* The power center is not someone who sits on a shelf, waiting for something to open up ahead. This person has made rapid strides, moving significantly every two or three years. The movement may be lateral as well as vertical. If the person has moved from one substantial responsibility to another, the chances are good that he or she is on a power track.

- *Consistently expanded responsibilities.* Give some people a duchy and they wind up with a whole country. They develop the resources and the influence to build empires. Look for people who expand outward.

- *Attends meetings.* There are some people who seem to be invited by the powers to almost every meeting, even though the subject matter being discussed may have little to do with their responsibilities. Management regards them as valuable resources in decision making and planning. Such people may not have much line authority; their power is derived from their closeness to those who have.

- *Signs memos.* In one organization, the personnel manager began to sign memos about policies and procedures that might otherwise have been issued by top management. His power had been delegated to him by the chairman, whose values he shared. People who ignored or crossed him later found themselves shunted into less important positions or terminated.

- *Has up-to-date information.* There are people in organizations who always have the latest inside information, which most other people, even those in higher-ranked positions, don't have. It's safe to conclude that such a person has access to a source of power.

- *Wins new projects.* A few people have their pick of new projects and enviable responsibilities. When a prestigious job opens up, the same people will be talked about as being in line for it. They are likely power centers.

- *Comfortable with power.* They talk knowledgeably about what is going on. They wear the mantle of responsibility quite comfortably. They relate well to other influentials. Gossip will tell you whether there is substance to back up this style.

- *Shelf-sitting.* People who take up space and mark time become obvious. They are ceremonial managers. In the case of a shelf-sitter, look for the real power. Probably the shelf-sitter is being bypassed—by whom to whom? Which subordinate is really running the operations?

Power watching is a matter of keeping your eyes and ears open to detect who has a record of accomplishment and continues to add to it; who has the substance of power rather than just the appearance of it; who acts as if he or she is on a power track leading to somewhere important.

Such people will be useful to you in building your own base of power.

Your Relationship with Your Boss

If the power center you identify with is your boss, you're very lucky. As you work to make your boss look even better in the organization, you can bask in the increasing glory.

But if your boss is not a power center for you, you are still advised to work to make him or her look good. A manager who is unhappy or suspicious about or jealous of a subordinate's relationship with influentials can make that subordinate's life pretty miserable.

Maintain frequent contacts and a close working relationship with your boss, even though you believe that you don't really need him or her, or that your boss doesn't make much of a contribution to your effectiveness. Don't volunteer information about your relationships with others; no need to rub the boss's nose in your successful networking and powerful friends. However, if the boss asks you about your conversations with others, talk about them without being indiscreet. What you want to convey is that you regard your outside relationships as quite the usual thing in an organization—nothing mysterious or underhanded about them. Certainly they are nothing that you will flaunt with anyone. Knowing people in power, you will be perceived by others, not only your boss, as having power yourself. Indeed, you do have opportunities to intercede for others and to drop names at opportune times. If it is in your interest to do so, fine. You'll pick up some IOUs for later.

Not only is it inadvisable to flaunt your relationships, it is equally unwise to take strongly partisan stances on behalf of your powerful associates. You want to be careful not to get involved in a shoot out. I'm not suggesting for a moment that you eschew all political activities. There's simply no way you can do that and remain visible in the organization. Just don't allow yourself to be labeled a partisan, especially if the conflict becomes polarized. If your "candidate" loses, so may you. You don't have to dissemble or manipulate. Indeed, you should not. But be discreet; don't make loud speeches and don't get tied irrevocably to one power center. And if you must make yourself a target, be nimble.

Above all, wear your associative power gracefully. You are, after all, borrowing it.

RESOURCES POWER

What do I have to offer that others need or want? That's the first question you ask yourself when building your resources power. And the second is, How can I convince those others that they can get what they want or need more readily, conveniently, inexpensively, and of better quality from me than from any others?

Look around in your own organization. People who have specialized knowledge or skills that are needed by other members of the organization are highly valued. As a young editor at RIA I learned that the staff professionals who enjoyed the most prestige and respect were those who specialized, say, in psychology, economics, and labor law. The generalists had much less identity and were referred to as "house writers." Turnover was great among them. In fact, being a specialist seemed to offer more job security—in the days when there was such a thing. It was a lesson that served me very well.

To be a generalist or a specialist is, I realize, a continuing debate. Recently, I heard a presentation by two training directors, each with a radically different orientation. Director A's company used outside contractors for the design and delivery of training programs. Director B's organization used in-house trainers for core programs and brought outsiders in for optional programs. Thus, Director A's primary function was to act as a go-between. When there was a perceived need for a certain kind of training, he searched the field and brought in an appropriate trainer.

Director B saw herself differently. She wanted to offer resources that were hers, and I understood her preference. She told of a call she had received from a division manager in her company in which the manager asked her to find someone who could give her staff a presentation on MBO. "No need," the trainer said, "I can do that." There was a suggestion of pride in her voice as she told the story, which I identified with.

Many of the old-time trainers functioned in the line before going into staff. If you ask them to put together a program on delegation, for example, they don't have to go looking for someone. They know what delegation implies. They've done it. I once argued with a young trainer in a Wall Street firm that he and his associates had never managed and couldn't call on their experiences to design and deliver management development programs. He shrugged and said that didn't bother him. His budget was ample for him to bring in the best experts. He was happy being a generalist.

As a generalist, people will rely on you to alert them to the latest trends and fads. They'll want your opinion as to who is a good resource in this or that subject area, who is an effective presenter, where they can find out something about whatever. The generalist is a broker, bringing in outside resources to meet inside needs.

The generalist points to his or her knowledge of human resources as a strength, even a source of power. But that source can be precarious. When budgets are cut and there is less money to retain outsiders, there is less need for a broker. In a decentralized organization, where managers can retain their own outside experts, the broker has competition. And in the minds of higher management there may be a difficulty in differentiation, as we say in marketing. To them, there may be a lot of potential brokers available. If we cut back this year, they reason, we can always find someone next year.

If you specialize, especially if you specialize in skills and knowledge areas that are vital to the continuing operation of the organization, you will probably enjoy a more substantial base of power. Perhaps the best role is to combine being a generalist with being a specialist in essential areas. And of course, your generalized knowledge of the human resources field will help you anticipate trends and solutions that might apply to your organization.

The information you have about what is available is a resource. Your ability to train in specific areas that are important to the operation is another resource. And resources that people need or want constitute a source of power for you.

Here are some considerations you might wish to ponder, in building your resources power:

- *What are some periodic or growing needs of your clients that you might become proficient in meeting?* Look at what your clients seem to need on a regular or recurring basis. Perhaps you've met those needs by retaining outsiders or bringing in various programs that were available at the time. Would it make sense for you to become qualified in delivering the program instead? Not only will you save money for the client, you'll be recognized as a vital asset.

- *What are some of the trends or changes in your industry, the economy, or the world situation that might create new needs for your organization?* You need to know your operation and the environment in which it operates. (This is a requirement for your competence power also.) For example, is your management moving toward new manufacturing processes, such as robotics? If so, begin now to determine the training needs. Will your organization be moving some of its operations to foreign countries? Training programs compatible with those cultures would need to be developed. Become accustomed to looking into the future to anticipate needs, which you can prepare yourself to meet at the appropriate time.

- *What are some of the trends in human resources that might suggest new and better solutions for your organizational problems?* As I've recommended elsewhere in this book, read the principal publications in the field. Go to meetings such as ASTD and American Society for Personnel Administration (ASPA) and Lakewood, sponsors of the annual "Training" conferences. If you can't attend them on a regular basis, at least read through the programs of the meetings. Analyze what the presenters are talking about. A lot of the presentations will be old hat, but you'll see certain new trends, programs, and techniques emerging. Do they provide a better way to approach the problems you see or anticipate in your organization?

- *What are some role changes you might make to be able to offer even more resources to your clients?* In some organizations there is increasing awareness of the value of internal technical or O.D. consulting. Would this be a sound strategic move for you? In some organizations in which there is increasing employee involvement, there is a need for people with facilitation skills. Should you become more skilled in group process? Do a diagnostic study on yourself to determine whether there are needs going unmet or being filled by outsiders whom you can replace.

- *Are you sure you are up-to-date on clients' needs?* Too many trainers wait for clients to indicate to them what their needs are.

Get outside the classroom. Use your network. Analyze the operation. Interview prospective clients. Look for any needs that you haven't been aware of. Eventually, as your clients and prospects become accustomed to seeing you in their territories looking for ways to be helpful, they'll start consulting with you, providing you with a chance to strengthen your alliance power at the same time.

• *How can you make your programs even more effective and important?* You're selling effectiveness. Your clients and trainees look to you to help them get more results. How can you increase the probability that they will indeed get more of those results? Look at your programs. Some of them may be generic or theoretical. Can they be made more practical? In my field of specialization, employee motivation, many trainers are still presenting conceptual and theoretical approaches to the subject, including reviews of Maslow and McGregor. Can you show your trainees how to apply those concepts and theories so that they can help to increase their subordinates' motivation and productivity? Furthermore, can you tailor your programs to resemble the real world in which your trainees work? In short, make the classroom walls disappear. What your trainees learn in the program should be readily and easily applied on the work scene.

The above recommendations are just some of the ways you can increase the value of the resources you have to offer. But you must also be prepared to market those resources and to practice your selling skills.

In time, when people in your organization think of training and consulting, your name will pop into their minds as a valuable resource.

ALLIANCE POWER

There is strength in unity. When I speak of alliance power, some people may wonder whether I'm suggesting that they organize a potentially subversive group. I am talking about an informal organization, but one designed to promote what its members believe is the well-being of the organization as a whole.

Such an informal group can exercise much more influence than any of its individual members.

One of my training groups provided a vivid example of this truth. A number of years ago, I was part of a team that was training branch managers of an organization over a period of several months. Initially, many of these managers complained that the home office didn't respect them and that they felt quite powerless to influence home office executives.

During the months of training, the training class coalesced into a true group, very supportive and collaborative. One bright manager came to the conclusion that there was no reason for the group to disband back on the work scene. The other members agreed with him that it was to their continuing benefit to meet occasionally to talk about their management problems, much as they had done in the classroom.

The group obtained permission to meet periodically on company time, although they had to assure management that it was important for them to do so in order to retain the learning of the classroom. It wasn't long before the branch managers realized that they represented a threat to home office management, and they decided to exploit that threat in a constructive way: They would bring their problems to the attention of the home office as a group. Heretofore, managers had done so individually, usually with disappointing results. It's easy to ignore or put one person off—but it's not so simple to ignore a whole group.

The first time the whole group sent a deputation to the home office, they found that the executives there were much more receptive to what they had to say. It wasn't necessary for the group to strong-arm, make threats, or deliver ultimatums. The fact that it was no longer individuals but the entire branch manager group was enough to instill respect in the home office executives. Relations between the home office and the field became more respectful, if not necessarily more cordial, than they had ever been.

Finding Your Allies

You have at least two sources of allies: other human resources professionals and managers and clients within the organization.

As was certainly true with the branch managers I wrote

about earlier, you, as one staff person, may feel that you lack clout, and your perception may be accurate. But what are your chances of linking up with other human resources people in your organization? Let's say you are a trainer, and that there are other trainers in your central or corporate group as well as in your branches or divisions. Possibly you've never spoken with one voice before when it came to human resources policies and methods, organizational needs and plans, or strategic directions and objectives. Surely as professionals you have something valid to say, at least when it comes to your areas of expertise. It may be easy for higher management to believe they can safely ignore the opinions and suggestions of one person, but it's difficult to justify turning backs on what a whole department or group says about this or that matter.

Of course, in some organizations any group may be deemed subversive or a pressure group, at first. You can reduce suspicion at the outset if you observe the following precautions:

- *Go through channels.* Stepping outside the established chain of command makes almost everyone in management defensive—and suspicious. You are "loyal subjects" even if you dissent. Whenever as a group you communicate with management, be obvious in your respect for rules, protocol, and tradition.

- *Keep communications positive.* Your human resources group may believe that certain practices in the organization are counterproductive. But rather than saying "We should stop this," suggest an alternative: "We should start doing . . ." Be positive and future oriented. Management gets nervous when people talk about problems and causes and the past. They relax when there is no hint of faultfinding and finger pointing. Your message should be "Here's a more productive alternative to what we have, and here's why we believe so."

- *Talk about what is observable.* Describe conditions as you see them and the results that flow from them. Try never to suggest that certain attitudes or motivations have led to such conditions. Your suspicions about what you can't really see can be disputed, but what you see cannot, even though others may have different perceptions.

- *Never overstate problems.* Even though your group may feel that solving a problem or filling a need is critical, never forget that you should be perceived as a professional alliance and not as a bunch of zealots. Passion threatens too many people. In making presentations, written or spoken, to most managements, I would rather risk slightly understating my case than overstating it. When emotion seems to dominate a proposal, people tend to back off, even in our more tolerant age.

- *Stick to problems in which you are perceived as expert.* That's where you have authority and credibility. It isn't as easy for management to dismiss your analyses or conclusions as it would be in areas in which you have no special knowledge or ability.

As an alliance, operate openly: no secret communications or private meetings. Everything your group does should testify to the fact that yours is not a hostile, subversive group, but one fully and obviously devoted to bringing your resources to bear on promoting the welfare of the organization.

In addition to the other professionals in the organization, you'll find many managers to be a source of alliance power. When you are pushing a change, an idea, a new policy program, or a project, you'll undoubtedly find managers who will join with you in promoting your "product." In most cases, I predict that if your alliance comprises not only professionals but managers as well, you'll enjoy even more clout.

Your clients and former clients constitute yet another source of group power for you. These are people for whom you have performed services. You already know something about how they feel and think. Presumably they already know something of your values. As you serve clients, incorporate them into your loose alliance. They can help you in your proposals to top management, in persuading recalcitrant prospective clients of the value of what you have to offer, and generally in moving the organization toward the vision you have of it.

Maintain close and continuing contact with clients. I was shocked to hear a trainer mention that he had recently been in contact with a manager for whom he had done a program six years before. Six years? In my view, he shouldn't have let even six months go by without some contact, some offer to help, or at least some expression of interest in the manager's operation.

Recently, a well respected training director, in describing the characteristics of a trainer whom she would be willing to recruit, talked about a "service orientation." Trainers, she explained, must think of themselves as providing services to their organizational clients and be enthusiastic about doing so.

Be service-minded. Look for ways to provide help and favors for your co-workers. But don't neglect to see these people you have helped as potential allies who can help advance your ideas, promote your projects and programs, introduce change, and generally reinforce your image as an expert professional in your field.

Using—and Preserving—Your Power

Building alliance power is an ongoing process. You'll want to preserve the base you've already built while strengthening and adding to it. If you are not very experienced in engaging in political activity, you'll find the following recommendations helpful to you in using and preserving your base.

- *Collect your IOUs.* Create on a continuing basis, obligations on which you may want to trade at some time in the future. For example:
  — Support a colleague in a meeting.
  — Perform extra service for a client, over and above what you agreed to in your contract.
  — Make yourself available to a client who has an urgent need on short notice, even rearranging your schedule to accommodate him or her.
  — Introduce people who want to meet each other or who would find each other interesting or helpful.
  — Write congratulatory notes after promotions and offer your services to make the new responsibilities more bearable.
  — Send memos supporting other people's causes.
  — Offer to intervene and mediate in a conflict.
  — Support a colleague's bid to head up a committee, task force, or project.
  — Offer to provide discreet help to someone who is having performance problems.
  — Let it be known to key people that you are accessible to

them and eager to help them in any legitimate way you can.

— Offer to assist a colleague in his or her presentation to management advocating a project, a decision, or some kind of innovation.

Don't forget the steps you have taken in building your reward power. The people you have recognized, supported, praised, and reinforced are your potential allies. If they indeed have felt rewarded by you, they will be happy or at least willing to return the favor.

At the risk of sounding callous and cynical, I urge you to look for ways in which you can do favors, large and small, for others from whom you might expect a favor yourself some day. Observe the powerful people in your organization. They never lose sight of the fact that they can benefit from allies. And the way you enlist allies is to make it beneficial to them to become so. Be aware of the benefits you have to offer—and remember when you have offered them. The name of the game is politics. Some human resources people disdain politics, but it simply is not realistic to do so if one wants more power and influence.

• *Use your IOUs carefully.* Don't go to the well too often, overusing the help of any individual or group. Keep "call ups" to a minimum, confining them to really important issues. Backing from your allies is in limited supply. It must be carefully conserved so that it is available when you need it most. Remember also that people who become too identified with you because they support or intervene for you eventually lose their impact on others, who believe that those allies will usually think your way. For greater influence, your allies should be seen as objective and as thinking on their own.

• *Make your requests in reasonable proportion to others' debts to you.* If you enlist people in a course of action they believe in, it's easier all around. When you take the initiative in pressing an issue regarding something that you are an expert in—such as policy or training programs or an O.D. intervention—they are likely to follow your lead because they see you as a formal leader. But it is unwise to ask an ally to make a major commitment by publicly taking sides on a controversial issue, as a payback for a relatively small favor. Maybe the person owes you one, but save it for a lesser matter.

There may be times when you want to put a bit of pressure on. If the other person is deeply indebted to you, you are in a position to say "I really need your help on this one. I'd like to ask you to join in supporting me, even though you have some reservations about it."

If the other person seriously disagrees with your position or the issue that you're supporting, be gracious about it. Back away. Make sure the other person knows that you respect his or her stand on the issue, and that you hold no grudges. It's possible that the other person will be sufficiently appreciative of your grace that he or she will feel further obliged to you.

- *Don't commit your allies without their approval.* If you are planning to quote them or use their names in connection with a move you are advocating, let them know in advance, get their okay, and keep them informed of the progress you are making.

- *Let your allies know what roles you expect them to play.* Perhaps you only want to use their names. But perhaps you want them to assist you when you make a presentation or introduce your idea to a group. Don't assume the other person knows what you expect. One way to engender ill feeling— and lose an ally—is to criticize him or her for not taking action that you believed the ally ought to have taken but didn't say anything about.

- *Avoid lost causes and disastrous victories.* Don't sacrifice your credibility and your power base for issues that virtually promise to be defeated or that require an unreasonable price. When you are considering a political shoot out, make sure it is not going to end with a carpet of "corpses," including those of your allies. Power plays should be aimed at building rather than destroying, and your moves should always be undertaken with consideration for the situation of your backers.

- *Be a graceful winner.* Push for what you believe is a reasonable victory—and stop. Some people become emboldened by partial success and decide to shoot the works. You want to achieve your objectives, which don't include devastating the people who oppose you. When you win, maintain friendly and supportive relationships with your erstwhile opponents. It should be as if the controversy or campaign had not existed. If you are sensitive to the feelings of people who resisted your project, you may find that next time some of them would like to be on your side. In organizational politics, being a good winner is as essential and desirable as being a good loser.

• *Keep your options open.* Some of your allies will want to enlist your aid and support for their projects and causes. Don't commit yourself unnecessarily. The fewer commitments you have, the freer you are to operate. Listen sympathetically to someone who wants to enlist your support, but be wary about saying yes unless you honestly believe you have something to gain. Of course, there will be times when you are on the fence, and a good ally will pressure you. You'll have to decide whether to commit yourself despite your reservations. In other cases, you can give support while retaining a fairly low profile.

One warning: If you cannot join with an ally on an idea or project, be up front about it. If you hem and haw, and hope that your indecisiveness will be accepted, know that most people will not appreciate it. They'll generally be more accepting of an honest expression of difference of opinion. You cannot build a power base when your potential allies wonder whether they can trust you because they can't seem to pin you down on a position.

Over the long haul, there must be credibility for there to be power.

REWARD POWER

Often when I ask a group of trainers whether they have reward power, the first answer is "Sure. We can give certificates showing that trainees have completed their training or demonstrated skills."

You can have much more reward power than that. When people respect your judgment, they will be gratified by your praise. I saw a clear example of this a few years ago when I was asked to subcontract with a small team of trainers who were going to deliver a management development program to a large, complex organization. The contractor, a well-known consultant, had already conducted a brief, pilot version of the program for one department, to test its feasibility. The mini-version worked, so we were now to train throughout the whole system.

The consultant took our small team on a tour of the trained department as well as the two other departments that had not yet been trained. The differences were immediately perceptible. We noted the enthusiasm of the supervisors who had been through the program and the accomplishments that flowed from their new knowledge and skills. They pointed out the changes they had made and the improvements that had resulted. Their subordinates seemed quite cheerful and friendly. The housekeeping was immaculate. The team spirit was obvious.

In contrast, employees and supervisors in the two departments without management training were somewhat standoffish. The atmosphere seemed less friendly. Housekeeping was dismal.

It was plain to see that the initial training, although brief, had worked a small miracle. But what was equally plain to see in the trained department was that the consultant's tour was seen by supervisors as a recognition of their achievement: the successful applications of the skills and knowledge they had gained in her program. As we walked around, she commented on this or that aspect of the operation, and people beamed. They saw the consultant as showing them off to the new training team. Their pride was a joy to see.

The consultant had enormous reward power. Her recognition of their achievement was of significant value to the people who had been through her program.

What to Reward

It's important to understand that the value of your rewards depends greatly on the esteem that others have for you. In that sense, your competence, professional, and associative powers can contribute much.

Look for clients who have:

• Solved a problem with skills learned from your programs or with your consultative help.

- Achieved significant success as a result of training.

- Been effective in systematic and systemwide application of techniques which you trained them in.

- Worked through conflict, with your assistance.

- Clearly demonstrated the benefits of the training programs you have delivered.

- Effected substantial change programs with your help and guidance.

In determining who is eligible for your recognition, give preference to those who have achieved results from the training or consulting rather than to those who have simply given themselves and their subordinates over to your training. Results and outputs are more impressive.

Also, be discriminating. The rewards must be seen as counting for something, as based on real achievement. They must be deserved. Be sensitive to the possibility that your rewarding one client may be perceived as putting down another. For example, client A accepted your training, and manager B did not. It's fine to reward A for what he or she has accomplished as a result, but you must take care that your language does not veer into a nose-thumbing to manager B. You want to encourage others to follow suit, not punish them for not having done so. Avoid, therefore, any "See what you missed out on" messages.

An even more sensitive issue is whether other prospective managers could have chosen the training that prompted your recognition. Some managers might have been constrained by their bosses and unable to become your clients. If you employ extravagant praise for the managers who were free to work with you, you may injure your relationships with those who had no freedom in the matter. Years ago, as a young manager, I sent a memo throughout the department lauding certain editors who had achieved quotas. One man who hadn't, felt very wronged. He was unable to meet the quota because of certain duties he had had to perform, which the others cited had not had. My lack of sensitivity had led me to commit an injustice.

In short, make sure that your praise for one person will not generally be interpreted as being at the expense of another.

91

How to Reward

Here's a concise guide to what makes rewards most effective:

• *They are deserved*. And others must understand why. Otherwise you look as if you might be favoring people who work with you on their training and discriminating against people who, for some reason, don't.

• *They are proportionate*. Again, the praise must be seen by others as fitting the accomplishment. Trainers have to be careful that they don't go overboard just because what is achieved is very important to them. When in doubt as to how much enthusiasm and praise are proportionate, better to understate than to overstate.

• *Be tactful*. Always remain sensitive to the reactions and feelings of others. Learn to ask yourself, How will others feel about this?

• *Be consistent*. When anyone deserves your recognition, give it. You may get very busy and skip some worthy person. That person may never forgive you.

• *Be timely*. Usually this means giving praise or some other kind of recognition as soon as the accomplishment is evident. Let too much time go by, and the news is old hat. People wonder why you are making a fuss. Your recognition will not only fail in its purpose but erode your prestige.

• *Be specific*. Make clear to everyone just what is being praised. General and non-specific comments are nice, but they don't have the impact of details. The more specific you are, the more likely that other prospective clients will want to sign on for the same service.

• *Use the language of equals*. Everyone writing a memo or letter of praise must be careful not to use condescending language. It's so easy. Trainers, in particular, must be sensitive to any implication in their language that the manager being praised followed the trainer's advice or had the good sense to take the training recommended. The more associative, professional, and competence powers you enjoy, the greater must be your sensitivity. Make sure your words clearly convey the message that you are complimenting a peer, a colleague. You are congratulating your equal, not your trainee or client. We trainers often need to remind ourselves that humility works wonders. What we're praising is, after all, someone else's accomplishment, even though we might have played a role.

Here are some of the kinds of rewards you can bestow on deserving people in the organization:

- *Letters of testimony, with copies.* Write your client, detailing what you think is admirable about what he or she did, and perhaps how it was done. Make sure that the copies you have routed elsewhere—to the client's boss, to the CEO, or to the director of human resources—are listed on the bottom of the letter for the client to see.

- *Letters from above.* You might persuade someone at or near the top to write the letters of praise, such as the president or the CEO. Then you explain to the delighted recipient, "I was telling Henry the other day about your success, and he was immediately interested."

- *Being used as a model.* Client A has achieved a significant success from your counsel, training, or consulting. When you sell your product to others, tell them of A's success. In sales it's called a verbal-proof story. Or do as my friend did in my opening story: Take prospective clients to A's department and let them talk with him or her. When you submit a proposal to other prospects, use the A story to show how you plan to proceed with them.

- *Assisting in presentations.* I refer to two kinds: sales and training. When you are selling to other clients, especially groups, ask your successful client to join you and give added authority to your claims. Or you might invite your client to be a lecturer during a portion of the program.

- *Articles in the house organ.* In partnership with the client, write an article showing what was done and why it was successful. If the training program, consulting, or intervention was not only successful but different or novel enough to be of interest to other professionals, plan a presentation around it at a conference of those professionals, and invite your client to share the platform. It seems to me that there is too little of this these days. Back in the early days of O.D., I used to hear a lot of presentations by both internal and external consultants in tandem with the line managers who had been their clients. In ASTD, my impression is that there is far too little of this. In fact, the complaint I often hear is that most of the presenters are external consultants and too few are in-house people with good stories to tell.

- *Word of mouth.* Your recognition doesn't always have to be formal and elaborate. Talking about the success among your client's peers will be appreciated. What you say will get back to him or her.

- *Advanced training.* Imitate the graduate seminar. Arrange a program for the "advanced" clients, something that carries a certain amount of prestige. Extend the invitation to an entire level of people. Your "stars" will shine among their peers.

In time, as your power and prestige grow, you'll find your clients and potential clients eager for your endorsement and reinforcement. That will make your work easier. People will listen seriously to what you have to say and offer.

But don't forget to reward your own staff. Remember that some of your power flows from them, too. They're easy to forget, to take for granted. Years ago, I, who constantly remind managers of the need to positively reinforce and reward subordinates who do a good job, had a rush job to delegate. I gave it to the one man on my staff I knew would not disappoint me. He did it, well and on time. The next morning he passed me in the hallway, smiled, and said, "You're welcome."

All of us need reminding.

PROFESSIONAL POWER

It is possible to build power within the organization by investing your time and energy outside it. You can acquire credentials, prestige, the endorsements of other professionals, and additional skills and knowledge, all of which you can use to increase your power and influence within the organization. Some of the many ways human resources professionals improve their internal standings are getting involved with academia, being active in a professional organization, becoming a presenter or a consultant for other organizations, being a leader in community and volunteer associations, and publishing.

Academia. Become a student or teach. Most organizations these days have a tuition refund program and will, depending on the relevance of what you study to the organization's operation, refund some or all of the cost of your schooling. A good friend of mine was employed by a large bank for several years. She managed to get the bank to pick up most of the cost for her MBA in finance and for her certificate in financial planning. Subsequently, she moved to a Wall Street firm and qualified for tuition for her Series Seven studies, which led her to her stockbroker's license. Then she enrolled herself in a Master's program so that she could learn more about the use of computers and video in training. She now has a total of three master's degrees (she had picked up one in education years before the bank experience) and enjoys tremendous prestige among her corporate training associates.

Many trainers who could avail themselves of tuition refund programs don't—to their detriment. Many people coming into training don't have an academic background in organizational behavior, organization development, or instructional technology. They receive most of their training after they become employed. Such in-house training may provide them with a very narrow professional base, one that they could easily widen by persuading their organizations to sponsor more education for them.

Perhaps you don't feel the need to gain one more degree. There are other programs of limited duration and narrow scope, from which you can get certificates. Many colleges and universities offer short-term programs in subjects of interest to you. Your professional, trade, or industry association may also offer limited seminars and workshops that could build your prestige. The AMA is an old favorite, with a name recognized by everyone.

In short, there are innumerable opportunities for you to increase your credentials through training, development, and education. Some of them are not expensive. And probably most of them will qualify for organizational sponsorship and assistance.

If you have the education and experience in the human resources field, you might be eligible to become an adjunct professor at a local college or university. You can teach a course or two, probably at night when it will not interfere with your work schedule. Most managements tend to be very impressed with academia, and you'll enjoy some of that prestige.

You may look to present at various professional conferences or before the AMA. In ASTD, the organization with which I'm most familiar, there is the annual national conference, although the competition to present at it is fierce. Each of ASTD's nine regions also has a conference, for which you can submit proposals. And there are more than 140 chapters looking for programming ideas and presenters. Your name will appear in the conference program or a brochure, along with that of your company, and everyone ought to be happy. Incidentally, if you're an in-house trainer, many ASTD units will welcome a proposal to present from you, since many of their proposals come from outside trainers and consultants. Too few come from insiders talking about what goes on in their oganizations.

Professional Organization. While in what follows I talk about ASTD, the organization I know best, what I say applies generally to other associations, such as ASPA and National Society for Performance and Instruction (NSPI).

At both the chapter and national levels, there are leadership and committee positions to be filled. Especially at the chapter level, ASTD is always looking for qualified volunteers. Look at your involvement as an opportunity to market yourself. Does that seem cynical and self-serving? It may, but you do have a right to try to take advantage of every opportunity open to you. But if you are entirely self-serving, you will defeat your purpose. People will soon spot you for the opportunist you are and push you aside.

Through the years, I have used ASTD to market Tom Quick. I have always been open about it. I became president of the New York Metro chapter of ASTD because it seemed useful to my career to do so. For some years, I'd had a problem of credentials. People in the training field tended to view me as a writer, not as a trainer or consultant. I've always thought that William Faulkner's slur branded me: "Those who can, do. Those who can't, write about it." By early 1982, I knew I would be leaving RIA, probably to go out on my own. But I also knew I couldn't live on my writing, even though I had done several books. I made myself available to be president of ASTD's largest chapter, because I believed I could persuade people that, by doing so, I was capable of doing stand-up training and consulting.

My strategy paid off. During the two years I was president, people simply assumed that the chapter's president must be qualified in the field. I began to pick up contracts largely through word of mouth and the publicity I generated throughout the training community by being president. Although I had written any number of books and articles, nothing accorded me more prestige than being the New York chapter's president.

Similar opportunities are available to you in your own ASTD chapter. But you must be prepared to invest the time to do a good job. Otherwise, people will judge you to be either incompetent or totally self-seeking. I've found that memories are short when it comes to hardworking people but very long when it comes to incompetents or non-performers.

At the national level of ASTD, there are committees and leadership posts on the board of directors. Again, much depends on how much time you wish to invest—or your organization will tolerate.

Before you decide to become active in your professional organization, you must have a "contract" about it with your employer or boss. Make a realistic assessment of the time you plan to spend with, say, ASTD, and let the boss know that. Otherwise you may run into difficulties and embarrassment with both your boss and ASTD. Obviously, if your manager begins to wonder where your priorities are, or if you are unable to function in your ASTD post because you have underestimated the time necessary, the result could be frustration and grief.

Time isn't the only part of the contract. You may have to do a selling job. What will the organization get from your involvement with the professional organization? Publicity, of course. A better professional; after all, you'll be in the mainstream, staying current with the trends and developments in the field. A potential manager, because you'll be learning managing and organizing skills in your chapter activities. (Actually, better managing skills than most, because you'll be managing volunteers, a much more demanding challenge than directing people in a paid reporting relationship.)

If you don't have access to a chapter of your professional organization, form your own. Many associations have criteria for chartering, but you could always have an unchartered group, or a satellite chapter of an established group.

Learn how to get publicity from your position in the chapter. What you want to demonstrate to your management is that you are esteemed by other professionals in the field and, therefore, your management should appreciate you.

Presenter or Consultant. This is an addendum to the preceding. If you have a good story to tell—about an innovative and successful program in your organization, for example—let it be known to your professional, trade, or industry association. Perhaps local service clubs would be interested in what you've achieved. Write about it. (Advice on writing coming.) Be willing to give speeches about your success (provided, of course, your management gives permission). It's good publicity for you and for the organization. And they'll probably appreciate having a celebrity working for them, a celebrity who trumpets the organization as a great place to work. The AMA might be interested in engaging you to give a portion of someone else's workshop or course that might be relevant to your experience.

In a few cases, successful internal human resources people with a track record have arranged with their managements to do outside consulting for one month a year, or 20 percent of their time, or one day a week. Why should the organization go for this? For one thing, it may be the only way they are going to keep their outstanding practitioner. For another, the experience the consultant gains on other contracts can be useful at home. Naturally, the salary is cut proportionately, but the outside consulting fees usually more than compensate for the loss.

Community or Volunteer Leader. Some organizations are happy to have you visibly work with United Way or on the Mayor's Task Force or for a charity such as a hospital or the Muscular Dystrophy Association. The organization comes off as civic minded, and you not only gain visibility but valuable contacts among the others working with you on the project.

The more responsibility you have on the committee, fund, task force, or project, the more people you can include in your network; the more planning, organizing, leadership and other valuable skills you can acquire (probably more than you can on the job); and the greater the opportunities to get your name published in the newspaper.

The fact that you are associating with some high-level, well-known figures in the community will add greatly to your prestige within the organization.

Publishing

Publishing is an excellent way to gain visibility, increase others' respect for you, and enhance the acceptability of your credentials. Writing a book is an impressive achievement—and I'll deal with that in the next section—but if you'd like to start out in a less onerous fashion, think about writing an article. Writing about human resources you'll find your best market to be professional magazines or journals, or business monthlies. Many of these publications don't pay for the articles they publish, but that isn't the main reason you're submitting your article. You want to be noticed. You want authority. You want credibility. You'll get all three and more with a well-written, well-placed article.

You can increase the impact of the original publication by obtaining permission to reprint or by purchasing reprints from the magazine or journal. Distribute the reprints when you give presentations or when you communicate with people with whom you'd like to increase your standing: other professionals, your organization's management, potential clients, or others.

Since even a well-crafted article of a thousand to two thousand words can take up a lot of time, find out before you begin whether there is a market for what you have to say. Send a query letter to the editor of your target publication. Keep it short; generally speaking, a one-paragraph description of your theme and treatment is adequate. Define your audience: Who in your view will most appreciate the article—technical skills specialists, management developers, human resources people, senior trainers, junior trainers, new entrants to the field? The editor can then make a decision as to the suitability of your piece for the particular publication and whether it will appeal to a sufficient number of its readers.

If the editor is interested, he or she will send you a card or a form letter, usually, inviting you to submit your draft. You'll probably get guidance as to its length and format, and the style that the editor believes is appropriate to the publication. Take the guidance seriously. The more closely you follow it, the better the chances of your seeing your name in print.

In most cases, you'll be invited to submit your article "on spec"—on speculation. The editor assumes no responsibility for accepting it. The risk is entirely yours, except that you at least know that the editor is interested in your idea. And expect to wait a while for the reaction; six weeks to three months is not an uncommon response time.

For human resources people, there is a sufficiently broad market for articles. I've published in all four training publications: *Training, Training News, Training and Development Journal* (ASTD), and *Trainer's Workshop* (AMA). There are *Personnel Journal* and *Personnel* (AMA), and other publications. Chances are you receive publications pertinent to your field or specialty that would welcome hearing from you. Editors are always looking for good ideas.

Editors are also looking for copy that is well written and doesn't have to be heavily edited. As an experienced editor and writer, I offer some suggestions that might make your article more acceptable when it reaches the editor's desk. First, get to your main point early in the article, preferably in the first paragraph. Editors groan when they realize that they have to figure out what you want to say and then rewrite your lead. Second, keep your sentences short, thereby avoiding the run-on, convoluted sentences that amateurs and some academicians think are impressive. The shorter your sentences are, the more likely that they will be clear. The greater your clarity, the less work for the editor.

My third recommendation is that you talk your way through your article. Read it aloud. If it sounds like you talking to another person or to a small group with which you've established a good rapport, it will have much appeal to the reader. Most of us are far more interesting and persuasive when we write as we talk.

Two more points will enhance the editor's interest: One, use words of common usage. We human resources people use lots of jargon. The less an editor feels the need to translate or define your terms, the better. Two, make liberal use of subheads. Every few paragraphs, use a subhead to describe a principal point you are about to make in the succeeding paragraphs. Subheads—and short paragraphs—help people organize and understand your material.

Each time you get an article published, you're exposing your name to thousands, perhaps tens of thousands, even hundreds of thousands of readers, depending on where the article appears. *Working Woman,* which has published some of my work, has a circulation of 850,000. One word of caution. Many human resources professionals have fantasies of their work appearing in the prestigious *Harvard Business Review.* Publication there would give any name a boost. But competition in *HBR* is very keen. Through the years, I've heard many professionals say they were working on an article for *HBR.* My impression is that almost none of them succeeded to publication.

Once you've become moderately successful in writing articles that get published, you may turn your thinking to producing a whole book.

Should you?

Writing a Book

A book with your name on the cover offers a great deal of prestige. Even if it isn't very good, most people will grant you a lot of points for the effort, which to most people is too formidable for them to contemplate. A published book also gives your ego a tremendous boost. To walk into bookstores and see your name on the shelf—well, that's a thrill denied most people.

Unquestionably, there are other rewards to writing a book. The fact that you know enough about your subject to fill two or three hundred pages can undeniably help to establish you as an authority. People are more ready to believe that you know what you're talking about. It's gratifying to have your opinions readily accepted. As the number of your books grows, so does the receptivity of others to what you say.

If you are achievement oriented, to use David McClelland's term, you'll get a boost from finishing a manuscript that you may not have gotten from other accomplishments.

There will be some fallout for you, in the form of invitations to speak, conduct workshops, and consult. A book can constitute a good marketing tool for you, although for it to be effective you may have to promote the book first. A useful way to keep the book's name before people is to have the publisher supply you with a one-page promotional piece describing it, combined with an order form. When you make public presentations, you can ask that the flyer be distributed to all members of the audience.

Initially, you'll want to have review copies sent to the publications in your field. Have a ready supply of books for sending to influentials, people who can spread your name about, or potential sponsors of your speeches or seminars. Ask your publisher's publicity people to arrange local radio and television interviews. And, of course, make presents of books to key managers in your organization.

If you get the chance, talk to an author who has already gone through the publishing and promoting process. You'll often get valuable tips for selling your book and keeping your name public.

So, yes, there are money, prestige, ego gratification, career advancement, and visibility rewards in having a book published.

But before you sit down and write a book, consider whether your expectations of those rewards are realistic. For most of us writing in the human resources field, money isn't much of an incentive. Our books don't earn much. And it certainly renders suspect any idea that writing a book is cost-effective. The average book in our field probably sells something like five to ten thousand copies. Even at the higher figure, you'll receive royalties of, say, $20,000 to $25,000. Sound like good pay? Figure out the time you spent writing it. Say that you spend ten hours a week for six months. That's a total of twenty-six hundred hours. That comes to less than $10 per hour, and may dip as low as $7 or $8. Not very good money for the time spent. The point is that most of us do not expect to get large amounts of money from our books. You simply have to ask yourself whether your time would be better spent, say, producing articles or developing new products, than writing a book.

There is, in my opinion, little to match the prestige and ego gratification that a book brings. But what will probably surprise you is that many people in the field won't even know you've brought out a book. Or if they know, they won't read it. There just aren't many serious book buyers in the human resources field. And there seems to be less and less money in budgets to buy books for personal benefit. But even if lots of people don't buy the book, you can gain visibility for yourself if you spread the word around. They don't need to read it to admire you. The title will look good on your résumé, too.

In summary, you'll probably achieve more exposure in articles than with a book or two. But as I've noted there are satisfactions from having completed a book that probably can't be matched by any other source.

If you have faced the reality but still want to do a book, here's some advice: *Do not write the book before you have obtained a contract for it.* If no one wants it, you'll have wasted an enormous amount of time. And no one will be impressed by your unpublished manuscript. Even if a publisher is interested in your manuscript, he or she may want extensive rewriting and reslanting. Again, you've wasted a lot of time.

Get a contract first. As you would in the case of a magazine article, write a query letter to those publishing houses you believe might be interested. There's an invaluable guide to publishing called *The Literary Market Place,* which you can usually find in a library. It will tell you who does what kind of publishing (you don't want to waste time with a publisher who never touches the kind of thing you want to write), the names of the editors, and the addresses of the companies. Your query letter should contain a paragraph or two describing the theme and scope of the book, its audience, and something about your qualifications. If the editor is interested, he or she will ask for an outline and perhaps a sample chapter or two. Based on the outline and the samples, the firm will decide whether to give you a contract. If the answer is yes, you can then proceed with the rest of the book.

If your book does nothing more, it will feed your self-confidence, which is an important ingredient in building personal power. You will have undertaken a tremendous project and carried it off. You'll have every right to feel good about that. And you've confirmed to yourself—and to others, you hope—that you have an area of expertise. You have demonstrated some competence, which is also a contributing factor to personal power.

But writing a book can do more. It can be an important element in your marketing portfolio. It may not sell you by itself, but it will help you to open doors and get attention. It will build your credibility. It may make you better known than you were before. It will, if you are fortunate, make you some money. Most important, perhaps, is that each book is a growth experience: In

103

the writing of it, you will be expanding your knowledge and your willingness to take risks by putting yourself in print.

Watch Your Back

The more you involve yourself in outside activities, even though you are convinced that your organization benefits directly and indirectly from that involvement, the greater must be your sense of caution. You may well be talked about by others, who will grumble that you are neglecting your inside responsibilities. Some recommendations that can protect you:

- *Be more than competent at your job.* When your outside work is sanctioned by management, you may be tempted to cut back on the work you do inside. But if you do, you open yourself up to criticism. Do everything you can to maintain as normal a workload as possible, to forestall criticism. What is just as important, be sure that you fulfill your boss's expectations of the results of your work. If the boss is strong, he or she will run interference for you. So your first concern will be to keep the boss pleased. If the boss is not strong, then you will have to protect yourself, and that will usually involve much time and effort to take care of both inside and outside obligations.

- *Keep your boss informed of your activities.* Yes, the boss gave approval. Don't make the mistake of assuming that approval endures forever. Conditions change. Pressures are applied. So do your boss the frequent favor of letting him or her know the wonderful things you are doing and how the organization will continue to benefit from them. Your updating meetings will provide reassurance for the boss and an early warning system for you if circumstances have changed.

- *Bring your boss into your activities.* Make your boss a hero, too. Ask him or her to come to meetings you attend or classes you conduct, or show him or her your manuscript and ask for an opinion or help. The more you involve your boss, the less you have to worry about his or her caving into pressure from others about the "wastefulness" of your outside interests.

- *Keep higher management informed.* If you are doing work outside that could be of significance inside, if you run across a new program or technique that might work for the organization, if you encounter a person who would be an asset on the payroll, let management know. Write brief reports or memos (with the permission of your boss, of course). Involving and updating higher management gains you visibility and affords you some protection from carping critics. It also reinforces the notion in management's mind that you are one great asset yourself.

Never for one moment forget that, despite the original contract, someone will come along and ask, "Why are we subsidizing him (or her) to spend all that time on other things?" Granted, you did a good selling job, once. Be prepared to do it again.

What if the organization does not share your sense of value and says no to outside activities? I hope they're paying you lots of money and offering you much growth opportunity inside the organization. But you also have to worry about the long-term effect of isolation. Are you learning more and more about less and less? The less cross-fertilization you have with the outside world, the lower your market value should you ever decide to move on to other opportunities. But before you decide to take the leap into the void, find out whether your organization might relent. Let them know how desperate you are to keep yourself growing professionally. They might be surprised, even pleased, that you want to become a greater asset, and give approval. If not, well, there are organizations that say yes to outside involvement.

AVAILABILITY POWER

"All I am," said an English aristocrat, "I owe to having been a quarter-hour beforehand." It's a bit simplistic, perhaps, but in it there's a great deal of truth: Being there before someone else, or being in the right place at the right time (even better when you're a bit early). Louis Pasteur made the famous remark, "Chance favors only the prepared mind." And a rock star put it this way: "I worked all my life to become an overnight success."

All of those statements describe an aspect of availability power, which is, essentially, being in the right place at the right time. Though sometimes it is just due to serendipity, many times Pasteur's belief is closer to the mark. Throughout my business career, many of the people who benefited from exceptional opportunities were not necessarily people of extraordinary ability. They were just there with the right qualifications when someone recognized a need.

Availability power is close to and overlaps resources power. But it differs from resources power in that it is at best a periodic thing. What is continuing is your general state of preparedness. In the 1960s it might have meant awareness of the Managerial Grid and Management by Objectives and the special cultural problems that forming conglomerates entailed. In the 1970s you needed to know about the new phenomenon of organization development and the surge of interest in customer service training. Even later, it would mean being alert to the growing emphasis on employee involvement, the globalization of our economy, Japanese competition, and the recognition of functional illiteracy. They all have human resources implications and significance.

Being prepared is the antithesis of being reactive. It means being generally aware of options, trends, and needs when they first manifest themselves. It might even mean you're saying to your clients, "There's something on the horizon that I think we ought to keep our eyes on."

You have to stay sensitive to the changes in your profession and in the political and economic spheres. You must develop prescience, an ability to predict.

People who stay up to date usually read a great deal. They follow their professional journals, business school publications (such as the *Harvard Business Review*), business newspapers and magazines (such as the *Wall Street Journal, Business Week, Forbes,* and *Fortune*), and their trade and industry newsletters and periodicals. They get themselves on the mailing lists for catalogues from publishers such as AMACOM (the AMA), Addison-Wesley, Dow Jones-Irwin, and John Wiley, to name a few. They stalk bookstores to see what is selling in the business section.

Prescient professionals attend professional, trade, and industry meetings and conferences, even spending their own money when budgets are tight. They develop extensive networks of people who might have useful information. They listen to vendors, because they know that salespeople often provide clues to new developments. And they understand that what others consider junk mail can contain further clues to what is being talked about and by whom.

Availability power is more than competence. It requires

knowing what you may have to develop competence in tomorrow. It means knowing where you can get help if you need it in a hurry.

Creating a Vision

An experienced human resources professional once said to me, "When you are a member of an organization, you should have a vision of that organization—what it will be, where it might go, what it will look like." So dust off your crystal ball and look at the potential of your organization. When it is actualized, what will happen to the function, the culture, the objectives of the organization? Look at the people who are influential. Where might they be likely to take the organization? Look at your markets or your client populations. What trends or problems are developing there, and how will they affect your organization's operation? Look at the economy, not only here but throughout the world, and the political situation. Look at all of them as they have impact on you and the people who work with you.

In addition to the more cosmic considerations, analyze these potential obstacles or opportunities:

- *Organizational changes.* What departments or divisions are to be phased out or merged? What new managerial or professional positions are being contemplated?

- *Staffing changes.* What internal expansions or cutbacks may be in the works?

- *Budget changes.* What monies are being included for the first time, or are being increased or reduced?

- *New facilities.* What new construction of a plant or a laboratory or branch might offer significant clues as to future priorities?

- *New projects or plans.* Will the launching of a new product or service line mean new demands on you?

No doubt you can find many significant indicators in what you see, read, and hear to help you to prepare for future contingencies. You'll find your influence enhanced considerably when a prospective client calls you on the phone and says, "We have a problem. Maybe you can find out what others are doing about it," and you can respond, "I've already been looking into that. When can we get together and talk about it?"

Of course, it's even better when you don't wait for the telephone to ring. Ask to meet with your clients to talk with them about some of the trends or emerging problems that you or they have intuited. If there is clear evidence that something needs to be done, offer to develop a proposal. Better yet, ask to develop a plan with the help of someone on the client's staff. Make it a partnership. You'll get the credit and have the satisfaction of knowing that everyone owns your ideas.

AUTOCRATIC POWER

As I write this, the announcement has been made that Henry Ford II has died. Ford presented a contemporary example of autocratic management, which flows from a unique relationship between the autocrat and the people who work with him or her. Henry Ford didn't tolerate competition with him in the company. He set policy, made decisions affecting the company, and he fired—almost at will.

We see fewer and fewer autocratic bosses these days, chiefly because most employees feel that they have options. They don't need to work in the arbitrary, restrictive, powerless work environments that often characterize autocratic management. There are at least four kinds of situations in which people are likely to tolerate autocratic power—or to have to. The first is the obligatory relationship such as exists between prisoner and warden. To some extent, the military is still autocratic, but less so than formerly.

A second situation in which autocratic power may be accepted derives from the unique situation of people being able to get something at the workplace that is valuable to them and that they are unlikely to get elsewhere, for example, employee-stock-holders of a company that promises to be successful and so make them wealthy, as represented by many companies in Silicon Valley.

A third example is what I term the company town. If you are the only or the principal employer in a town that is somewhat

108

isolated or distant from other places to work, you can get away with almost anything. However, Americans' mobility has vastly reduced the number of company town situations.

Finally, there's what I ironically refer to as voluntary servitude. There are charismatic and visionary entrepreneurs who make work so meaningful and exciting that people bond themselves willingly to it. They'll trade their freedom of action for the chance to do work that gives them satisfaction.

It's inconceivable to me that human resources professionals would seek autocratic power. The notion seems antithetical to the values that most of us espouse. For example, the development of human resources is abetted by providing more growth opportunities and chances for people to acquire more responsibility as they become qualified for it. Promoting slavish obedience doesn't quite fit our image or our styles.

But human resources people can benefit from autocratic power. As I write, I'm thinking of a vice-president of human resources in a large corporation that is largely controlled by one man. It's a highly centralized operation. The vice-president has almost immediate access to the chairman. When he discusses the company's training and development programs and policies, it's with the chairman. Obviously this person has much more position power than the usual human resources vice-president. He enjoys associative power. And if he can persuade the boss to delegate, he can acquire assigned/delegated power. A human resources professional can accomplish a lot with that kind of power. Unfortunately, what the autocrat says yes to today, he or she can just as easily say no to tomorrow. I would imagine that my friend the vice-president is an accomplished salesperson.

Sometimes in my presentations on power before human resources people, a member of the audience will assume that I condemn autocratic or authoritarian styles of management. I do not. Kurt Lewin, the famous German-American psychologist, defined authoritarian management as one of the three styles, the other two being democratic and laissez-faire. I firmly believe that it is a legitimate style, though probably not on a permanent basis. There are times when a manager should feel free to pull rank if he or she believes that's the way to get through a bad situation. When a manager confronts, for example, a confused, chaotic and demoralized work group, in which a great deal of destructive conflict exists or which poses threats to the health and safety of workers, it may be time for a temporarily authoritarian approach. Or, on a less dramatic scale, when the manager has specialized knowledge that workers don't share, during the time it takes the manager to impart this knowledge he or she can insist that everything be done "my way."

While I acknowledge that autocratic power can be legitimate, I've always found that, when confronted by it, I had low tolerance for it. I suspect that most human resources professionals share my distaste. But if it pervades your organization, make use of it.

CHARISMATIC/VISIONARY POWER

Webster's defines charisma as "a personal magic of leadership arousing special popular loyalty or enthusiasm" and "a special magnetic charm or appeal." I really don't know how one develops charisma, but I know firsthand the effects of charisma on people. I have worked with charismatic people. They are very exciting and inspiring. They do indeed arouse loyalty and enthusiasm. They tend to be visionaries, to see what the rest of us don't or can't envision. I suspect that most people who have had close experience with charismatic leaders will describe the experience as profound and moving, even though the followers may ultimately part ways with them.

I have never had an association with a charismatic trainer. It's difficult for me to imagine that most organizations would tolerate one. "Orthodoxy" and "compliance," two characteristics regarded as desirable for the bureaucratic life, are not generally in the charismatic's vocabulary. And because charismatics are often poor with details—they usually make terrible managers—they aren't going to be very good at meticulous planning of programs. Their appeal is as strongly emotional and inspirational as it is intellectual. Thus, the transfer of knowledge and skills from them may be erratic, perhaps more so with abstract concepts.

Is there a difference between personal power and charisma? I would hate to have to make a precise differentiation. Generally speaking, personal power is more frequent. In fact, I believe that many people can build personal power. Many people can command respect and convey confidence, competence, and authority. Charisma is not commonplace. The charismatic conveys confidence, competence, and authority too, but in addition there is excitement. When you associate with a charismatic, you feel that it is a special and unusual experience that most people will probably not have the opportunity to enjoy.

In short, charisma creates impressive power, but I don't know how one develops it, and I doubt whether it is suitable for a trainer.

However, many people can develop the related visionary power. You can develop a vision of what your organization can, and possibly should, be. You can have a vision of the consequences of your efforts to change your organization and improve its effectiveness. You can build a vision of your power, influence, and your own effectiveness. You can build a vision of leadership and the impact it can have on your organization.

I offer you some questions that might help you to create the vision that could guide and inspire you. After all, visioning or imaging is becoming quite a popular technique now.

- What are the promising strategic and operating plans of your organization that point to significant, exciting change in the way your organization presents itself to its customers or its constituencies?

- What are the projects in either the planning or executing stage that, if successful, may lead the organization in new and different directions?

- Who are the leaders that have tremendous potential to take the organization in new directions?

- What are the economic, political, and social trends and circumstances that offer opportunities and challenges to your organization?

- What would be the impact on the leadership, structure, and operation of the organization were you to implement the training and the human resources policies that you think appropriate?

- What do you think the organization would look like in two to three years if it were everything you believe it can and should be?

111

• What do you believe the organization should concern itself with less? more?

Often, we can get turned on by projecting into the future, establishing a vision, and then working backward to see how it might be realized. People who have a vision have a mission, and the commitment to that mission pervades all that they do. They have and convey excitement and enthusiasm. They may not be exactly charismatic leaders, but others find them interesting and attractive. And if those others wish to share that vision, then the visionary finds that his or her influence over others has increased substantially. The visionary has power to move people.

POSITION POWER

I've saved the discussion of position power for the last, chiefly because few human resources professionals enter an organization to occupy a powerful position. They work to create it, and they succeed in doing so by drawing on the other kinds or sources of power.

Four examples of human resources people who created position power come readily to my mind:

1. Fred H.'s company was seeking ways to improve productivity significantly. He designed an operant conditioning or positive reinforcement program, using Skinnerian principles. With his help, management established uniform standards throughout the company and trained managers and supervisors in feedback techniques to keep employees continually apprised of how close they had come in the given period of measurement to the standards. The resultant boost in productivity boosted Fred into a vice-president's slot, where he reported directly to the president. Fred illustrates how exceptional personal and competence powers can make the human resources position very influential. Given the effect of Fred's ideas on the bottom line, whatever issued forth from Fred's office was taken very seriously.

2. Stanley M. was recruited as personnel director. The CEO was new to his position and came to rely on Stanley for counsel, especially in matters of personnel policy. In time, Stanley virtually became the CEO's alter ego and assumed many high-level responsibilities not usually associated with human resources management. Many communications to the work force on policy issues were signed by the personnel director rather than the CEO. Probably chemistry played as much of a role as competence in elevating Stanley, but because of association, Stanley's position in the corporation became quite powerful. In time, Stanley became known for speaking for the CEO.

3. Teresa M. came to a large corporation with a Ph.D. and a distinguished record in both academia and consulting to the private sector. Teresa also had developed superb political skills. Before her arrival, the training function was fragmented, with a corporate department and semi-autonomous departments scattered throughout the giant company. She was able to persuade top management of the benefits of centralized training. In time, Teresa became a vice-president in charge of all training functions, with scores of professionals reporting to her. Since training was very important in her company, and since nothing happened in training without Teresa's involvement, however marginal, she accumulated enormous power for her position. In her case, personal, resources, professional, and competence powers played significant roles in making her position so influential.

4. Wally S.'s situation is similar to that of Stanley. He has become a vice-president in a corporation controlled largely by its founder. When he argues for or recommends a project or a program, he does it in the CEO's office. There is no middleman. Wally sets training policies, with the firm backing of the founder. Wally is competent, but perhaps the greatest contributor to the influence of his office is associative power.

As we've seen, high-level reporting is one way to invest a position with power. Being able to influence the bottom line, as in Fred's case, is another. Many of the most influential trainers, in my experience, think of themselves as helping to run a business rather than running a training department. They are partners with management. And I believe the partnership concept should permeate the human resources professional's thinking. I'm not suggesting that, if you are a training director, it is not important to build a strong, competent staff. It certainly is. Your staff should share your strict and high standards. But if you're going to build an empire, it must extend beyond your office and the classroom walls.

Some additional thoughts on using the other sources and kinds of power to increase your position power:

- *Competence*. Of course you know the human resources field. But can you diagnose what your co-workers need to operate effectively and then deliver what you promise? If what you say is needed is on target, and if you consistently deliver what you say you will, your credibility and that of your office will soar. And with the credibility will go power.

- *Personal*. Perception of power is probably the same as having it. If you are convinced that, as a human resources professional, you have some of the keys to greater effectiveness and higher profits, then that conviction will be conveyed in how you talk and relate to others. William Wiggenhorn of Motorola once told me that his CEO had mandated the creation of a "competitive work force." Even if you haven't received such a mandate, you'll project greater personal power if you believe that such is your mission and within your capability. No one else is likely to think of you as a person of power and importance if you don't.

- *Assigned/Delegated*. Do you know how to use your persuasion powers to pull down responsibility from above? Have you proved that when there is a special or challenging job to be done, you are the person who can be relied on to do it? Have you fashioned yourself into a crucial subordinate? Do you regularly look for work you can do that now isn't being done? Do you consider taking on assignments that others don't want because they are afraid of them? Do you seek ways to pull down tasks and responsibilities from the highest management level possible?

- *Associative*. Do you know the key people in your organization? More important, do you enjoy easy access to them? Can you call on the phone and get through? Can you ask for a meeting and get an early appointment? Do you seek more informal moments with them, such as at breakfast, lunch, or a drink after work? Do you know where the high power-centers are, and do you seek their occupants out often? Some judicious name dropping doesn't hurt, as long as it is discreet and not overdone. The more comfortable you are associating with the power people, the more others will assume you share their power.

- *Resources.* Remember that what others need and want should be part of your inventory. But you probably shouldn't wait until they recognize that need. Use your persuasion skills to lead them to the recognition that they have a particular need and that you are the person to fill it. Take the initiative.

- *Alliance.* If you need support for a project or an idea, are you confident that you could enlist it? Do you know which people share your values and your vision, respect you, and would join with you if you needed them? Do you have an informal organization of people with whom you trade information and supply help? There is strength in numbers—have you built up yours?

- *Reward.* Your job doesn't end when the training is over. You need to follow up the training to see what changes and improvements occur as a result. Then you reward the client who was so intelligent as to follow your recommendations, and you spread the word that this is one exceptionally competent manager. The implication is that if others want such beneficial results, you can deliver—and create more visibility for them, as well.

- *Professional.* Are you creating a professional reputation among your peers outside the organization that can find its way inside? Do your co-workers think that if your professional colleagues hold you in such high esteem, they ought to regard what you say and do more seriously? Have you, through writing and speaking, achieved a celebrity that reflects well on your organization?

- *Availability.* Have you demonstrated that you are ahead of your—and most others'—times? That you have anticipated needs and developments? When people are looking for an exceptional person or group to do a tough job that they aren't sure how to do, do they think of you or your staff?

- *Autocratic.* While an authoritarian style is usually not one you'd seek, if it prevails use it to reinforce and strengthen

115

your function. The closer you are to that autocratic power, the more of it your position will enjoy.

- *Visionary.* If you have a vision of the organization and share that vision with your co-workers, you'll soon find yourself regarded with new respect and acceptance. If your vision is attractive and realistic, others will buy into it.

One question that often comes up in my presentations is, What do you do with a relatively powerless boss who is just content to hold on to his position and not much more? If your boss is a shelf-sitter, you'll find it even more imperative that you foster relationships up and across lines of authority. You can't afford to be identified with your boss's relaxed and casual attitude. In time, as you draw on other sources of power, practice the fine points of persuading, and produce effective programs for clients, your co-workers will come to understand where the real human resources power resides.

Will your boss feel threatened? Possibly. You can't entirely avoid that possibility, but you can reduce it by strengthening your relationship with the shelf-sitter. Talk to your boss. Discuss your plans with him or her. Perhaps you don't need your boss's input, but it costs you very little time to make him or her feel needed and respected. In time, as the human resources function becomes more valued because of your work, the boss will enjoy the new prestige and may be less likely to interfere with you or resent you.

YOUR POWER ACTION PLAN

The following is a little quiz to help you assess how many of your power resources you are drawing on, and where you should put more of your efforts in building and maintaining a power base. You may be surprised to find that you are not using all of the sources or kinds of power that are available to you.

KIND/SOURCE OF POWER	USING SUFFICIENTLY	COULD USE MORE
Competence	☐	☐
Personal	☐	☐

KIND/SOURCE OF POWER	USING SUFFICIENTLY	COULD USE MORE
Assigned/Delegated	☐	☐
Associative	☐	☐
Resources	☐	☐
Alliance	☐	☐
Reward	☐	☐
Professional	☐	☐
Availability	☐	☐
Autocratic	☐	☐
Position	☐	☐
Charismatic/Visionary	☐	☐

If you have a strong power base, nine or ten of your choices will be in the "using sufficiently" column. If you do not—and I suspect that most human resources people don't—then you must look for ways to strengthen that base. Chances are very good that if you are candid with yourself, you are not using the power that is available to you. Of course, it takes planning and building. Look down the "could use more" column and select a kind or source of power that you are not drawing on as you might, one that is feasible for you. Develop an action plan for doing so.

One way to plan your action is to use what in journalism are called Rudyard Kipling's servingmen: why, what, where, who, when, and how.

Why is assumed in your choice. You need power, and this kind or source is there for you to develop.

What kind of power is at the present time most feasible, most readily available?

Where can you find this power? In what department? What function? What activity? Through what contacts?

117

Who could be involved in helping you to acquire more power? What clients? What managers? What specialists? What outside people?

When is the most opportune time for you to draw on this source of power? On formal occasions, such as training? Informal occasions, such as chats, lunch, or organizational functions?

How will you accomplish your strategy to add to your power base? What specific steps will you take?

When you've accomplished your action plan, pick another source of power and develop it. Or, if you feel very ambitious and impatient, make plans for more than one assault simultaneously. It's an ongoing effort. You will never be justified in believing you have all the power you need. Because people and events will be chipping away at your base. You need to continue to add to it and strengthen it.

BENEFITING FROM POWER

Putting it quite simply, the more power you have, *the more options you enjoy.* You'll generally find people more receptive to your ideas and proposals. Your requests for money, staff, equipment, and resources will get a more serious reception. You'll find you have greater latitude to initiate and to experiment. You'll have more control over your work and your planning. Other people will make room for you. Power equals freedom, since both mean that you have more choices.

The more legitimately powerful you become, *the more results you'll be able to obtain from others.* People will want to be associated with you. Anyone on the power track is perceived as a winner, and people like to be close to winners. People will hope that they can increase their own power by their proximity to you, just as you have probably benefited by your relationships with other powerful people in the organization. Since, as a power person, you have more resources and influence, people will want to work jointly with you because they see a greater chance that their projects will be approved if you are involved. Your associates will be hesitant to turn down your requests, to ignore your recommendations, to fail you if they suspect you have the power to make life troublesome for them.

Power brings you *more control of your life.* You know what you need and want—from your work, the organization, your career, and others. Knowing what you want and where you are going is an important early step in building your power base. You increasingly call the shots, as you go up the power ladder. There is less sitting by and waiting for others to tell you what you must do and what you are permitted to do. You gradually acquire more control over your progress, your direction, and your objectives by eliminating, or at least reducing, the constraints that organization and authority have placed on you. Each time you are successful in removing a constraint or surmounting a barrier, your increased power makes others more reluctant to try to constrain you.

Whether or not people like you for being powerful, *they will respect and perhaps admire you,* as long as your methods for building that power have been ethical and non-manipulative. Of course, your power must truly be substantial and not based merely on an impressive style. The more power you accumulate, the less likely it is that others will be fond of you. They may even fear you a bit. But they're not likely to ignore your recommendations. However ambivalent they may feel about power, they will admire you for having become as influential as you are.

Your self-esteem will grow with your power. You have pushed out your boundaries, taken risks, and assumed control of your life and career. You have every right to admire yourself, as long as your acquisition of power has been honorable. You're bound to be an interesting person.

4

What Makes an Effective Trainer?

In developing a list of the adjectives that describe an effective trainer, I've drawn from the ASTD compendium of competencies, as well as from a composite profile of the training professionals I've admired through the years. You'll quickly note that the underpinnings are effectiveness and credibility. I seriously doubt whether a trainer can enjoy one without the other. If you're not effective in getting the desired results, who is going to pay attention to you? And if people don't believe that you can do what you promise, you'll encounter any number of obstacles to effectiveness.

The following list isn't an exhaustive one, but even if not complete, it's a good place to begin.

HONEST

Good trainers, which is synonymous with effective trainers, are strictly what they are. They don't pretend to be what they're not—though there's plenty of temptation to be. An in-house trainer struggles to be a generalist and worries that having to say "I'm not experienced in that area" to a manager seeking help will seriously erode his or her credibility. Are you asked to do some team-building? Why not? Well, if you haven't had much experience with group process, that may be a very good reason not to. A facilitator with inadequate training in process will do an incomplete job at best, and at worst could be responsible for serious damage through being unable to recognize and intervene in damaging behaviors of participants.

On the consulting side, there is the lure of good money. I've known consultants and trainers who presented themselves as equipped to take on kinds of work for which I was sure they had no credentials. One man I knew sold himself as a sales trainer, and the only selling he'd done was in getting business for himself. That's sparse training for showing others how to be effective with prospects. Incidentally—perhaps fortunately, for any potential client—he wasn't very effective in selling himself. Another consultant once called me to say that she had just landed a contract to train managers in motivating employees and would I please lend her one of my books on motivation so that she could design a program. To my knowledge, she had never done any training in employee motivation and productivity. In both of the above cases, the concern apparently was "Get the contract first, then worry about the delivery."

The issue of honesty is even more subtle. One freelance trainer boasted about a two-hour presentation he had made, for which he charged a great deal of money. I was happy for his instant prosperity, but I couldn't hide my dismay that his talk covered an area in which he was not expert. For that much money, I suggested, he had passed himself off as a specialist. He denied that he had misrepresented himself, although he acknowledged that the sponsors of the talk had assumed he was indeed an expert on the subject. He just hadn't done anything to discourage that assumption. To him, the question of ethics was not relevant, because the talk, to use his description, had been a success: "They liked what I gave them."

Perhaps. But he didn't give them a first-rate presentation, which I hold that the fee demanded. He couldn't, and he knew that he couldn't. Perhaps no one else knew that. But I have a problem with passing oneself off as being more knowledgeable than one is. So should the less-than-candid presenter. Secure in the conviction that others will not know enough to detect the deception, a trainer may unwittingly not succeed in it. The result is a loss of credibility, for the person and maybe for the rest of us in human resources.

It takes courage to admit one's limits, to say, "No, I'm not an expert, but I'll get you one," or, "I can do a decent job for you, although it's not my field of expertise," or, "No, that isn't my specialty, but I'd be happy to bring in an associate who is an expert and who'll work with me."

Being aware of what you don't know or do well is an important step in professional growth and in the subsequent increase in your value to your organization and clients. Admitting it is an important contribution to your credibility with them.

TOUGH

One of my favorite stories involves the CEO who called his vice-president of human resources in one day, handed him a copy of *In Search of Excellence*, and said, "Do this." As absurd as the story is, it isn't foreign to any trainer or personnel veteran. Granted, there are some among us who would have smiled, taken the book, and given an answer equivalent to "Yes, boss." That doesn't mean that they would have done anything with the notion. That much idiocy they might have avoided. But a responsible act would have been to challenge the CEO to tell them just what "this" meant.

We trainers are frequently described as reactive. We deliver what we're asked or told to deliver. Worse, we are sometimes accused of designing programs that will *please* or be *acceptable*, rather than what will change behavior. Ideally, we in human resources should see ourselves in the business of selling effectiveness to our clients. We should, I believe, put our expertise on the line to help our colleagues and clients to do a better job.

I say *ideally*. The worst example I ever saw of a trainer caving in occurred in a medium-size corporation that had never before had a training department except for its field salespeople. The new trainer interviewed all the managers who were to go through the initial program, about fifteen in all. Her informal diagnosis showed severe problems of morale, communication, resentment toward and distrust of top management, mutual suspicion among peers, and other indicators of distress.

Her program could have been a major intervention, with opportunities for group work to break down some of the barriers, for the participants to talk about their real-life difficulties and obstacles, for top management to establish a dialogue with the middle-tier inhabitants. But that didn't happen. The design she chose was very safe: time management, leadership theory, individual

125

exercises, and quizzes. It is true that she would have encountered some fear and resistance in top management had she insisted on a realistic agenda for the three days. But then she would have been doing her job, living up to her commitment as a professional. As it was, her bland program simply engendered cynicism in the participants: Management, they were convinced, had little or no respect for them, to expect the middle managers to accept such pablum. And the training manager came under suspicion of being manipulative, of using the informal interviews to con the participants into believing that she would truly be responsive.

It takes courage to stand up for what we believe to be true. It's not easy to say to management, "You're not going to get the results you and the organization want if you continue to do what you're doing," or to level with a manager who wants a non-productive type of training: "That's not going to get you what you want. I'd prefer not to waste our time and your money." It's a matter of integrity to tell management that the programs they want you to deliver will not be cost-effective or perhaps effective at any level. But trainers can't hope to build clout without projecting competence and authority. While it's true that managers must take responsibility for the training of their people, we must take responsibility for what we recommend and design. Our attitude should be that if it won't work or do what the manager wants, we have no business wasting time with it. Trainers who just "go along with it," especially when they should know better, do not serve themselves or the human resources profession well.

But we live in a world that isn't always logical. Suppose you've said to a manager who has proposed training you do not recommend, "That's not going to do the job you want. Let's talk about what has a better possibility of getting you the proper results." Let's assume further that you get a negative reaction. What recourse do you have? You might try the assertiveness-responsiveness approach I described earlier in the book. For example, "John, let me describe to you what I see happening. You are consulting me as a resource in training. You want me to deliver a program to some of your people that I am certain will not do for you what you want it to do. Even though I've given you my opinion on that, you keep urging me to ignore my conclusion and give you the program anyway. That distresses me because you're asking me to do something against my better judgment.

What you want will be costly in time and money, which I believe will be wasted. Can you imagine how upset I am at that prospect?"

John—unless he is a complete rotter and replies that he couldn't care less—will probably say that he can imagine. Follow up responsively: "I've told you what I see happening and how I feel. Tell me what you see from your perspective and how you feel about my conflict."

With luck, you've created the chance for a dialogue. John may actually be willing to give you a chance to explain in greater detail why you are opposed to his idea and, better, what you think is a more effective alternative.

Of course, John may be a rotter, and insist. You'll have to decide whether to decline, or go to higher management (in which case you'll probably totally alienate John), or deliver the program under protest. If this is where you decide to draw the line, threaten to quit. But at least you'll know that Andrew Grove wasn't talking about you in the *Wall Street Journal* article that opened this book.

RESPONSIVE

To be effective, a trainer needs to respond to the varying needs and concerns that trainees bring with them. Of equal importance is the trainer's recognition that the trainees bring experience, knowledge, skills, and insights with them into the training room.

There are at least three components of responsiveness. One is empathy: being able to identify with trainees' situations, feelings, and motives. Your perception of the value and effectiveness of your program is not nearly as important as their perceptions. Once you know fairly well where your trainees are coming from, you're in a much stronger position to know what to offer and how to offer it. One of the best trainers I ever worked with as a subcontractor used to spend much time telling those of us who would be training with her how the trainees saw their jobs and respective positions in the hierarchy, what frustrations they had in functioning in the organization, and, to the extent possible,

127

what some of them were trying to achieve. This woman had done extensive homework, to be able to talk with trainees confidently about their world and how they saw it. Not surprisingly, this woman began to achieve credibility with the trainees almost from her opening remarks.

Another component of responsiveness is active listening. You want to hear what trainees are saying as well as detect what they are leaving out. Often in the classroom the instructor proceeds along a preconceived route and tolerates interruptions. But the experienced trainer knows that interruptions, arguments, and resistance tell you something important for you to know. It's a good idea to regard every comment or question by a trainee as potential feedback for you. Are you reaching them? Are you helping them? Are you being accepted by them? Most trainers will read this section nodding, perhaps impatiently. The temptation may be to think, "Let's get on to something new." The problem is that so often the more we know, the longer we've been training, the greater is the possibility that we do not listen carefully, that we assume we know what the trainees are telling us without having to pay close attention. How many times have I set out to answer a question or to respond to a statement only to find, after a time, that I have given an irrelevant or inappropriate response. Active listening means to stay alert, and when you know what you're doing, you think you can do it in your sleep. And you may.

Finally, there is humility. A friend of mine who is not a trainer but who has wide contact with people in our field surprised me by complaining one day about the condescension she detects in many trainers when they talk with her. I'm not sure where the arrogance that she senses comes from. It may stem from the hours trainers spend in front of trainees, pushing the latter through the designs that the trainers have created and are familiar with. You can recall meeting trainers who seemed to have an authoritarian manner: "Listen to me. I know what I'm talking about." Their message to trainees may be, "I am here to teach you. You have little or nothing to teach me." Our power in the classroom is enormous. We can use that power to exercise control, that is, to guide the group to a predetermined objective. Or we can abuse that power to dominate the group, to put our stamp on everything the group does and thinks.

INTEGRATED

The good trainer—one who gets results—is knowledgeable about all three components of adult learning: content, methodology, and process.

Content is the subject matter. It's what you deliver.

Methodology is how you deliver the content—through lectures, group discussions, exercises, role plays, or visual aids such as overheads, slides and movies, and interactive video.

Process is what goes on among the trainees and between them and you. Process refers to the nature and dynamics of the interactions.

For many years we trainers have been burdened by a general perception that we are more concerned with the delivery of a program than with what is delivered. Our critics say that we fuss with our visual aids and graphics and varied formats without exercising sufficient critical control of what we present. Certainly in the years in which I have been active in ASTD I've seen numerous instances in which speakers with appalling or simply trivial ideas have received high evaluations because of the slickness of their presentations or the warm rapport they established with audiences. I've also witnessed unfortunate events at which speakers with less refined platform skills received poor ratings despite the excellence of their ideas.

Content is the trainer's product, not the presentation of it. The primary questions we must ask of content are does it meet the needs of the trainees and will it be perceived by them as meeting their needs?

The methodology you use depends on the nature of the content, the time available, the composition and size of the group, and the atmosphere of the training environment. The correct methodology enhances the delivery and the learning.

Process seems to be the component of learning that trainers as a group are least comfortable with. But ignoring or being unaware of process could lead the trainer to permit barriers to learning to arise and to fail to take advantage of a very important learning resource—the group. In any newly formed aggregate of trainees, before a true group forms, there will be resistance to the training, authority issues, role competition, power plays, and so forth. The trainees may bring resentment and skepticism into the classroom. The trainer may initially have little credibility with the group. People tend to play the same roles and maintain the same relationships with others in the room that they demonstrate on the work scene. Some trainees will vie for power. All of these process matters have impact on what goes on among the trainees and between the trainees and the trainer.

A high priority for the trainer is to help the trainees get beyond these initial behaviors and relationships to start building a true group. When they entered the room, at least some of the trainees had learning objectives that related to the content. But as the members of the training class coalesce into a group, the learning objectives of the program become those of the entire group. Members of the group will apply their respective resources— knowledge, experience, skills—to help all members achieve the group's learning objectives. The group will deal much more effectively than the trainer can with members who are impediments to the learning process through anger, hostility, resentment, negativism, or indifference.

The effective trainer, therefore, values all three aspects of adult training: sound content delivered effectively, with appropriate attention paid to process.

IMAGINATIVE

It's fairly easy to take a program that has already been designed and apply it in your organization. It's quite different to take a theory or a concept and translate it into a program that meets a specific need in your company. This takes imagination, a quality that the ASTD competency study describes as "intellectually versatile."

The trainers I have most admired in my twenty-five years in the business are those who showed imagination, who searched for ideas that they could translate into practical reality. They're not afraid to strike out in new and often untried directions. Early in the 1970s we were already hearing about self-directing work teams, a radical new approach to productivity, especially in the U.S. To institute such experiments took not only imagination but courage.

I encountered some very good examples of innovation

when, in 1971, I did research for my first book, *Your Role in Task Force Management*. The benefits of using temporary problem-solving groups such as task forces and project teams were not widely appreciated in American business at the time, except perhaps in high-tech organizations. There wasn't much information that told managers how to form, run, and use them. Yet, I found some examples in which human resources specialists, sensing a particular need for an adaptive, temporary group to handle problems or projects, had fashioned some innovative structures that paralleled the permanent, functional organization.

Before quality circles became fashionable in this country, a friend of mine created similar groups among supervisors in his company. The groups were to solve problems and provide training for their participants. The idea was known, but the translation into reality was my friend's accomplishment, one that showed much innovation and imagination.

I sense that many trainers are not imaginative and innovative. Perhaps they have little encouragement to be so, since there is such a variety of programs available today. Few people feel the need to pioneer. Pity.

PROFESSIONAL

I recognize that there are thousands of human resources professionals who do not see the need to be active in, or even to belong to, organizations such as ASPA or ASTD. It's a regrettable fact, especially as far as training is concerned, since so many enter the field without training credentials. Actually, the training field is unusual. People who become trainers often have never had the ambition to do so. They've come from education, social work, line management, and selling, to name a few typical sources of trainers. One veteran trainer put it humorously to me: "One day they're unemployed teachers. The second day, with a new job, they're trainers. And the third day, they call themselves consultants.'

A slight exaggeration. But the fact is that many trainers have come into their jobs with little or no background directly related to training, with the exception of classroom skills. They have no theory base. Often they don't know how large organizations function. They can't speak the managers' language.

One of the ways a new trainer can learn about this constantly evolving, increasingly complex field, and one way a seasoned trainer can stay abreast of new developments, is to be active in ASTD. And to attend its conferences and others like it, such as Lakewood's annual Training event. And to read the principal publications in the field, such as *Training and Development Journal, Training,* and *Trainer's Workshop.* There are any number of books relating to training that are available through ASTD, Masterco Press, and most bookstores, and are published by such publishing houses as John Wiley, Addison-Wesley, McGraw-Hill, and Jossey-Bass—to name a few.

But back to membership in ASTD. I believe it is very important for the training professional to contribute to his or her field. Those of us in it are usually not perceived as professionals, with reason. We must change that. One way to work to change our image is through the organization that represents us on the national scene. Whatever its flaws and deficiencies (for which we trainers must bear some responsibility), ASTD represents us, speaks for us, is our identification, and is our vehicle for change. Trainers who disdain membership in ASTD are, in my view, cheating themselves, the rest of us, and the profession they want most to build. (The same comments apply to membership in ASPA.)

INVOLVED AND INFORMED

It's hard to understand how some trainers can consider themselves competent when they know very little about how their organizations operate or about the environment in which they exist. A good trainer is involved with and knowledgeable about the mission and the operation of the organization he or she is a part of. After all, it's the trainer's job to help the organization's people be more effective in achieving the organization's goals. You can't really know how to fill that job until you understand the needs of your clients, what they're charged to do, and the world in which they function. You can't judge the effectiveness of a training program until you can envision how it can improve the skills and talents of the members of your corporate culture. You can't hope to make an impact on your organizational system until you understand what it does, what it is trying to do, and how it can be helped.

Although you are the trainer, you participate in the learning process. To be effective, you must be perceived as part of the organization.

To create closeness with the trainees, to establish yourself as a participant in the learning, isn't easy. Trainees will usually perceive you as an authority figure, different from them—so different, in fact, that they will resist your training, at least in the beginning. In my view, the key to creating a shared situation is to let them know that they are equals, though not, at the moment, through knowing what you know. They bring to the classroom resources, strengths, knowledge, and perspectives that the trainer must respect. Trainees will become partners in the learning process only if the trainer permits and encourages it. The group will adopt the trainer's objectives as their own and will work as a group to accomplish them, enhancing thereby the trainer's efforts.

ANALYTICAL

All you have to do is to look at the large crowds at national conferences such as those sponsored by ASTD, ASPA, or Lakewood to know that many trainers are curious and growth oriented. The conferences are large shopping centers for techniques and ideas, but therein lies a danger. I'm often persuaded that attendees are looking for attractive solutions rather than appropriate solutions. They're not always sure of the nature of the problems for which they want answers.

Flip through the evaluations attendees make after presentations, and you'll come away with the distinct impression that judgments are often made based on the reaction of the listeners to the presentation rather than to the applicability and transferability of the speaker's ideas. The evaluations usually concentrate on the format, the packaging, and the smoothness of the presentation.

A question trainers frequently ask, even before they know very much about what a consultant or trainer does, is "Who are your clients?" I've found that if you drop enough well-known names quickly, you're more likely to gain an audience for what you can do. No matter that what you did for the "brand names" may bear little resemblance to what their needs are. The question invites hype.

A trainer's analytical skills need to be more incisive and thorough. It's not enough to be open to new stimuli, or shop for the answer to "What's out there?" One must take into account the specific needs of the organization: How is this concept or technique or program going to help us reach our objectives and realize our vision? What needs will it meet? Is there a better way to obtain what we need and want?

The program being audited may be flashy, provocative, colorful, novel, and may have already been adopted by other users, but none of these distinctions constitutes a guarantee that it will work effectively for your organization.

Answering the questions above requires not only a broad knowledge of human behavior and the human resources profession but also a detailed awareness of the culture, direction, and operation of the organization. Matching theory and practice requires well honed analytical skills.

INFLUENTIAL

Good trainers make an impact on their organizations. They know how to influence the executives and managers with whom they work. They not only know their product, they are expert at selling it. Such trainers project an image of personal power. This derives in large part from their confidence in their ability to define problems or opportunities and to work with management in developing solutions or ways to capitalize on opportunities. They are innovators in their organizations, not simply people who take and follow orders from on high. They have departed from the stereotypical image of the trainer as follower to assume the mantle of leadership.

ENTHUSIASTIC

Not long ago, I walked away from a panel presentation by three successful in-house training directors, feeling dissatisfied and let down. Their presentations had been mildly interesting, and the trainers were well grounded in the human resources profession. I agreed with their training policies and their perspectives on organizational change. Yet, there had been something missing from their presentations, something I believed should have been there. Finally, I realized that not one of the trainers had manifested any enthusiasm for the work he or she was doing. There was no current of excitement, no conviction that their programs would result in better management and a more effective organization. They were not turned-on people—they were people portraying themselves as doing a job.

Such were my perceptions, and they troubled me. I sat down immediately and wrote a short article that was published by the July, 1987 newsletter of the New York Metro chapter of ASTD. It is reprinted here with permission of the New York chapter.

> For years, I thought training was a boring profession. And I thought that most trainers were bored with it. They wrote that way, and they talked that way. Their articles in training periodicals seemed uninspired and uninspiring. Their presentations at conferences were dry and lacklustre. I was so unimpressed with what I read and heard that, although I was actually a member of the profession (as a vendor, preparing developmental programs for the Research Institute of America), I stoutly denied that I was a trainer.
>
> My perspective has changed. Well, part of it, at least. For one thing, I call myself a trainer. For another, I no longer believe that training is boring. In fact, I devoutly believe that training is one of the most exciting callings I could think of. But you still wouldn't know that from reading what trainers write and listening to what trainers say. I have the impression that trainers see their raison d'être in designing programs and putting butts on chairs—BOCs, as Chet Delaney might, with his lovely irreverence, put it. They write in the training journals about what they do and how they do it, and it often comes out dry and lifeless. Their presentations are correct but frequently produce a ho-hum effect in me.
>
> My passing uninteresting time is not what worries me. No, I think instead about the awful possibilities that many of these trainers who make it all seem boring talk and write the same way in their organizations. If my suspicions are on target, some of these people may be turning people off rather than turning them on to training.
>
> That would be a tragedy. Because, you see, I'm convinced,

135

after 30 years in organizational life, that training is the key not only to the health and prosperity of our American business but indeed to its very survival in our new globally competitive economy. There are a lot of executives and managers out there who don't seem to realize yet that we are playing in a new major league with some powerful teams. It's not enough for them to simply go along with training in the same half-hearted way as in years past. It's no longer the issue of how much money can we make regardless. It's *whether*, as our current economic landscape shows. There are wrecks and ruins all around us. And the number will accelerate.

There may be any number of reasons why American businesspeople are slow to get the message. But there's no acceptable reason why American trainers don't see and respond to the survival issue. The fact is, as any salesperson knows, we can't sell people if we don't seem sold on the product ourselves. Our product is survival and growth. And it's doubtful that American business can make it without what we sell.

So, how is it that, with such an essential product and lofty mission, we make it all sound grey and boring?

I suggest that we think—and feel—a bit more intensely about how important we are to our clients. And even if we are turned on ourselves, we need to keep in mind that we can't be very successful unless we turn them on. All in all, I prescribe a bit more passion for trainers. We need to make our work sound as exciting as it is.

5

Changing Roles and
Perceptions

"Training is too important to be left to trainers." That's a statement I've made in print several times, occasionally baffling or even enraging trainers who apparently believe I'm putting them down.

The fact is that management is responsible for training employees. Traditionally, managers have usually sidestepped that responsibility and placed it on the shoulders of trainers. It's very convenient to do so. If the training doesn't take, for any reason, blame the trainers.

Many trainers have participated in this arrangement and, when the training didn't achieve its desired effects, wondered why they had to take the fall.

This book has had as its premise that trainers can and should avail themselves of the power that is theirs to take. But my admonition accompanying that premise is this: No matter how powerful you become, how much influence you can exert in the organization, you must never forget that your clients, the organization's managers, have ultimate responsibility for the success of the training you deliver. And that is how it should be.

True, as I've pointed out, trainers are obliged to know the operation. They must have a sense of the concerns, the problems, the needs, and even the aspirations of the managers who engage their services. But it is improbable that trainers will ever know the conditions under which the managers work as intimately and as thoroughly as those managers. And, of course, it is doubtful that managers will understand the human resources development field as trainers do.

Because of the distance between the training department and the day-to-day responsibilities of managers, there is always the possibility that when trainers prescribe training on their own, they miss the target. Managers, prescribing on their own, may also do more harm than good.

Recognizing the problem, many trainers are beginning to leave the classroom and their offices to join in partnerships with their clients. Some have formed advisory boards, comprising functional specialists, managers, and trainers. Such boards diagnose organizational needs and recommend remedies. Some trainers ask their clients to join with them on a training committee when the trainers take on assignments in those clients' operations. Both approaches recognize that training is a joint operation, that trainers need the inputs of their clients in designing and delivering training, and that managers need to own the programs.

The accountability for the appropriateness of any training must be shared between the deliverer and the client. Where managers and trainers take such shared accountability, the training department is less likely to be viewed as a cost center and more likely to be seen as an active, indispensable contributor to organizational survival and health.

A second phrase I've quoted many times is "Managing is a function of training." A training director imparted that piece of wisdom to me twenty years ago. The essence of its meaning is that a manager's responsibility is to make sure that his or her work force is always effective. But since the conditions and the environment in which work is done are ever-changing, the manager is almost daily obliged to help his people to acquire the necessary skills, knowledge, and expertise to cope successfully with change.

The implications for the trainer arising from this premise are enormous. First, it is doubtful that delivering periodic training will do the job when the phenomenon of change is ongoing and continuous. Second, much of the training, coaching, and counseling that are required under conditions of unceasing change will also be ongoing on the work scene.

Consequently, more and more organizations expect their trainers to perform as consultants. In fact, in some organizations, the trainers now function almost entirely as consultants—diagnosing, intervening, and calling on outside training professionals to do the actual presenting. There is no question that trainers are well advised to acquire consulting skills, to be able to perform dual roles. Not many years ago, trainers were trainers and O.D. consultants were consultants. Now, the two worlds are melding.

Increasingly, much of the trainer's work will be experiential and designed for specific clients, which will be performed not in the classroom but in the client's department. Moreover, it will have satisfied our changing national educational and occupational needs. We are encountering a national literacy crisis, with large numbers of people entering the work force being functionally illiterate. Educational and training programs will have to be designed at primitive levels. Add to this the tremendous need for retraining due to the obsolescence of certain kinds of jobs and the introduction of new technology. This means that vast portions of the work force, many of whom are reading-impaired, need to be trained in new skills to stay employable.

These are exciting times for trainers, at least for those who are adaptable and flexible. American management, by and large, has been reprehensibly complacent about training, except where basic and technical skills are involved. Other kinds of training are usually referred to rather scornfully (or at least suspiciously) as "soft stuff." But the need for that "soft stuff" has become a hard reality. Those of us who function in supervisory and management development know that, overall, we have performed in a mediocre way, judging by results. The quality and effectiveness of American management leaves much to be desired. It simply is not world-class, in a global economy.

However the prestige and demand for trainers grows, the traditional problems remain for them. They are all too often seen as powerless appendages. To be effective, trainers must achieve and exercise the power and influence that are available to them in most organizations.

For the sake of everyone.